... Where the bad sad kids go

Alison Sutherland, Ph.D.

Sutherland, Alison, 1950 –
Where the bad sad kids go / Alison Sutherland

I would like to acknowledge the New Zealand Child, Youth & Family Research Access Committee for their permission to publish these anecdotes.

For everything there is a season, and a time to every purpose ...
                                                    Ecclesiastes 3:1

Where the bad sad kids go

A New Zealand Youth Justice Residential School experience during the late 1990s, based on my reminiscences as the school's teaching principal.

This book is dedicated to the young people who passed through the residential facility where I taught. I may have been the school's principal, but you were the teachers and I your student.

Aroha nui, Alison (aka "Miss")

CONTENTS

FIRST IMPRESSIONS

From the suburban street it didn't look like a kids' prison. Not that I should call it that. More a place where adolescents who have committed serious crimes are incarcerated. Nope, that's even worse. Incarceration evokes images of primeval dark dungeons, chains and cages. That doesn't fit the scene of the slightly shabby, single story building stretching across the spacious residential property in front of me. Not even a strand of barbed wire, locked gate or identifying sign in sight. But I know what this place is from the address. It's a residential facility for young people who have committed serious offences, and I was there to see if I wanted to apply for the position of teaching principal.

Driving through the open gates, I pass dilapidated tennis courts and a disused in-ground swimming pool. The main building is in front of me and I park my car in the visitors' carpark. Stepping awkwardly out of the car in my tight skirt, I grip my newly purchased black leather briefcase and walk briskly towards double glass doors leading into an administration area. The doors are locked. Behind these doors are another set of internal doors and behind these is a reception desk. There is a woman in a dark uniform sitting there, her back to the door. Banging on the window doesn't get her attention. Standing there, wondering what to do next, I watch a car coming up the driveway. It backs into the carpark next to mine. A gentleman gets out of his car, walks towards me, smiles, says good morning, reaches up and presses a gray button set high on the wall beside the double doors. Really! A female voice echoes through an intercom system, asking him his name and business. Following his response, a lawyer no less, there is a clicking sound and the doors slide open. Clearly familiar with the process, he enters the premises. Feeling rather stupid, I walk closely behind him and also enter the building. We push through the second set of doors and into the reception area. I introduce myself, am invited to take a seat, take a deep breath and wait. Perhaps 10 minutes later, a small woman, accompanied by a tall, hugely obese man, appears. She introduces herself by a name that I don't quite catch and invites me to follow her. Her male companion opens a door leading away from the reception area and the three of us, me in the middle, the man at the rear, walk through a long, rather dingy, narrow corridor. For a few metres I feel as if I'm in a dark tunnel, but the corridor opens out and on our left is a large bathroom. I glimpse a row of toilets without seats and a cubicle that perhaps serves as a shower. There are no doors or curtains. Continuing down the drab passageway we pass several cell-like rooms on the left that actually have doors. Doors with locks. On the right is an open area with two tired, grey couches that are severely stained and have stuffing protruding through the torn material. There is one old armchair, this one's brown, with an arm missing. An antiquated television set, minus knobs, is attached high up on the wall close to a very high, yellow ceiling. There is no other furniture in this depressing room. From these observations I deduce that this must be the boys' wing. The foul smell of stale sweat and body odour gives it away.

We make our way through the boys' lounge area, passing a few more cells on the left and some on the right. The woman stops and I stop close behind her. We are confronted with a locked door that separates the residential side of the facility from the section designated as the school. The small woman and I stand to the side while the overweight man squeezes past us and unlocks the door. The three of us step into a small, L-shaped corridor, then the man locks the door behind us. I resist the urge to giggle. I feel as if I'm in an 'Alice in Wonderland' scenario, only I'm Alison. Squashed together in this small alcove, I look around. As well as the entrance into the boys' wing we have just come through, there are four other doors, all within reach and all locked of course. The first door on the right, at the bottom end of the 'L' shape, leads to the outside world. This, I am informed, is the school personnel's private entrance into the school. The first room on the left, the size of a large bathroom, contains several antiquated, wooden school chairs and three obsolete computers that perch on small student desks. We shuffle forward. The next room on the left, only slightly bigger than the bathroom, is the school principal's office. The door into the office differs from the others in that it has no window. It is a large, solid, wooden stable door in two pieces, with a top and a bottom section.

Both sections have locks. This room contains a large desk, several chairs, a filing cabinet and a photocopying machine. There are shelves attached to the walls stocked with classroom materials. Across from the office is another small classroom that is littered with bits and pieces. I sight fragments of student desks, a yellow plastic bucket and a wooden frame. A box filled with used paint brushes suggests it may be used as an art room. The next door to the right, the one nearest to the schoolroom, is a kitchen. It harbours a relatively modern fridge/freezer, an electric oven, sink, bench and several cupboards with sliding doors. There is an open servery window between the kitchen and the schoolroom.

Following the woman, who uses her keys to unlock the stable doors, I enter the office and am directed to a chair facing a large window that looks into a very large, open plan classroom. The small woman, whom I had presumed was the school's principal, explained to me that she was the deputy principal of the nearby mainstream secondary school. It is her responsibility to oversee the Youth Justice Residential School. The much larger secondary school, referred to as the "attached school" was some kilometres away and so the Residential Centre School was almost autonomous, except for a monthly Board of Trustees meeting. Apparently the board meeting provided some means of accountability, especially in the area of the budget. Its members had little to do with the day-to-day running of the school. While the deputy principal had overall responsibility for the residential school, she didn't work on-site with the young people, the teachers or the residential staff. The teaching principal, two full time teachers and a teacher's aide were the only academic staff in the school. Together they provided educational programmes for up to 20 young people. The students were predominantly violent males, with the occasional female. The young people ranged in age from 14 to 17 years, although it was known for a younger child to come into the residential part of the facility temporarily, but not into the school. She warned one of the difficulties for the school is that many of the youth hadn't attended a school for months or even years. Most had a history of truancy issues and quite a few of the young people were virtually illiterate. She also warned that many of the young people had an 'attitude' about having to attend school while they were at the residential facility. Another major complication was that the young people were usually enrolled in the school for short periods of time. Some were only there for a few weeks, or even days, while they waited for a court hearing or decision. Others could attend school for anything up to four months as part of their sentence and this was sometimes rolled over to an even longer period.

Glancing over the deputy principal's shoulder as she talked, I watched as several scruffy looking boys pushed and shoved at each other, taking turns to press their face against what I hoped was a reinforced glass window. This window separated the office from the crowd hovering in the open plan classroom. Ignoring the escalating banging on the window, the provocative comments sailing through the air and the rattling on the closed office doors, the deputy principal continued with her explanations. While there was a maximum number of 20 young people catered for in the youth offending centre, for security reasons, only 15 were allowed to be in the attached school at any one time. Only 15? It looked like a mob out there. As she talked I tried to focus on what she was saying, but became distracted by all the people wandering around the classroom area. Intermingled amongst the boys were a few girls and more than a few adults, male and female. Turning to see what had engaged my attention, the deputy principal stopped her explanations to point out the school staff from the residential social workers. The latter were there to ensure everyone's safety in the school; students and teachers. I watched as several heavily built men unsuccessfully herded youth away from the office window. Already unsettled by the offensive hand signals and loud raucous comments, my mortification and anxiety levels intensified as wet tongues flicked out of mouths and licked the window. Thoughts of fly dirt and other filth being stuck to the glass washed over me. Nauseated, I tried not to retch as a ball of spittle dribbled down the glass and a grubby finger reached out and played with the foam. I turned my attention back to the lady. Completely ignoring the antics of the young offenders, the deputy principal returned to explaining her role in the facility. I jumped as a nearby telephone rang loudly. Smiling an apology at me, she picked up the receiver and greeted the caller. As she listened, her smile changed to a frown. With a few curt words she banged the receiver down, apologised to me, saying something unexpected had come up that she must attend to. She'd be back in a few minutes. With that she exited the office, closing and locking the bottom half of the stable door, while leaving the top half ajar. I was alone. But not for long.

Within minutes of her leaving, two young men jumped over the locked lower half of the door and entered the office. The tallest one grinned at me then turned away and began riffling through papers on the large wooden, cluttered office desk. Tucking a ballpoint pen into the pocket of his pants, he crossed the floor in front of me. Bumping against my knees he reached over, opened the top drawer of the metal filing cabinet and commenced flicking through some folders. I later discovered this filing cabinet contained records belonging to all the young people, past and present, who attended the school. The other young man in the office was of stocky, muscular build. Less friendly than his mate, he snarled at me to "get out the fucking way, bitch!" I looked away from him. Changing his focus from me he rummaged through the bookshelves secured to the inner office wall. Cluttered like the desk, the bookshelves held a variety of resources, including writing utensils and large sheets of paper. Feeling uncomfortable and more than a little threatened, totally out of my depth, I just sat there, flushing with embarrassment when the stocky boy leaned closer and barked "Boo!" into my face. His breath stunk. I continued to sit on the hard chair, feeling powerless and a little silly, like a child waiting for someone to come and rescue me. To my consternation, a couple of the supervising adults glanced into the room but didn't seem at all bothered by this youth invasion of the school office. Absolutely out of my comfort zone, I continued to sit quietly, waiting for the deputy's return, pondering on how I had managed to place myself in this situation of being surrounded by teenage violent offenders in a secure unit that didn't feel very secure to me.

So there I was, totally apprehensive (okay, scared), passively waiting for the woman to return and continue with the interview. The stocky young invader lost interest in his rummaging and approached me again. "What ya doing here, cunt?" he rasped. Startled and intimidated, I squirmed on the hard wooden seat. Before I could think of an adequate response, the deputy principal reappeared, growled at both the young men and shooed them out of the office. We chatted for a few more minutes, I asked a few questions and then it was time to leave. Thank goodness. Despite my reservations and against my better judgement, as the deputy escorted me back to the front office, I handed her the completed application form I had prepared earlier that morning. With a brief comment of farewell I hurried out to my car, never expecting to be interviewed for the position. But I was.

Having accepted a telephone invitation to meet with the Board of Trustees at the attached mainstream school, curious and nervous, I attended the interview. Phew. The interview panel knew what they wanted and after some intense questioning, I was sure it wasn't me. After an hour and a half I left believing that I, a European, middle-aged female would not be suitable for the position of teaching principal at a Youth Justice Residential School that predominantly catered for Maori male youth. Feeling somewhat relieved and a little deflated, I went home and consoled myself with a chocolate bar. Later that evening I received a phone call from the deputy principal who had interviewed me initially. As she talked about some of the issues that had been raised during the interview process, avoiding the main reason for the call, I found myself reassuring her that it was okay that I had not gained the position. Silence followed. "But Alison", she said, "I'm telling you the job is yours." Surprised, stunned, more silence. Then I found myself stuttering an acceptance. Hanging up the phone, I turned to my husband who was hovering nearby. "Guess what?" I said.

Before I began my new role as principal/head teacher at the 'Youth Justice Residential School', I thought it would be a good idea to have some knowledge of what I was getting myself into, so I turned to the Internet to conduct some research. What I found was that there were several youth justice residential facilities situated around New Zealand that accommodated offenders aged from 14 to 17 years. My stomach lurched a bit when I read, because of its secure status, the facility I was to work in was designated for those young people who were considered to be the most serious offenders. Oh great! Many doubts later, and a lot of helpful advice from friends and family, like "don't wear your jewellery to work" and "don't dress too provocatively", I arranged to meet the outgoing teaching principal and school staff to learn what the job entailed. What I learnt was that the Ministry of Education's 'Education Review Office' had written a scathing report criticising the school. It would appear I was joining a sinking ship.

THE BEGINNING

Teaching young criminals had never been one of my life's goals. As a teenager I visualised myself nursing the grateful sick and at the age of sixteen, applied for a Community Nurse training course. Many bedpans, soiled beds and night shifts later, a new career path seemed like a very good idea. Although it wasn't planned, I became a single mother, married, produced two more beautiful children and settled into domestic oblivion. It was not to last. Recovering from mental health problems linked to postnatal depression, I refused to continue with electric shock therapy. No longer wanting to anaesthetise myself with prescribed tranquillisers, gritting my teeth I flushed the drugs down the toilet. So began the journey to heal myself.

Disenchanted and bored with housework, isolated in our little bungalow with small children while my husband worked long hours, bored with the mindless fodder that daytime television offered as entertainment, I sought an inexpensive hobby that I could immerse myself in. Preferably something that would get me out of the house. An evening class at the nearby college was advertised in the local weekly paper. Having only attended two years at high school, with some trepidation I signed up for the Wednesday evening class offering School Certificate and University Entrance English. This small decision was to change the direction of my life. Loving the lessons and attending every class, at the end of that first year I was stunned and delighted to find that I had passed both School Certificate and University Entrance English. Encouraged by my English teacher, the following year, at the age of 26 I enrolled at University as an adult student. There are few words to explain how I felt that first day as I walked up those concrete steps towards my first lecture; trembling legs, and mixed feelings of inadequacy and wonder would be part of the description. Education and Sociology offered stage one courses that I could take without any prerequisite, and so my academic direction was set.

Two years later, a partial degree catapulted me into teacher training and a career in Education. I loved it. But what an emotional roller coaster, balancing a career and a young family. Late nights and early mornings creating what I hoped would be interesting lesson plans, studying during any spare time that came my way so that I could keep up to date with my teaching. Setting the alarm at 4 am gave me three hours of study time before the family arose. Adrenalin rushed through my veins as I stood in front of classes of secondary school students and attempted to convince them I knew something that was worth them learning. I would not describe myself as a popular teacher (a survey in one school where I taught showed popular teachers were those who were young at heart, trendy, had a sense of humour, and were 'fun'; I scored pretty low on that popularity list), but I did, and still do, perceive myself to be an effective teacher. This self-belief was reinforced when senior students, motivated to achieve, clambered to enrol in my economics and computer classes. Having a rather serious and stern demeanour (I understand my nickname was 'Darth Vader'), rather than seeking to be liked, I strived to be fair. I suspect this is why the majority of youth who were considered to be 'behaviourally challenged' were well behaved for me. Moving up the school hierarchy, I was promoted to Dean of the junior school. Several years as Dean and senior teacher in local, co-educational state schools led me towards the position of Head of Commerce at a prestigious girls' school.

It is my experience that one small step often leads to something bigger. From Head of Commerce I was seconded to the New Zealand Stock Exchange to direct their 'Stock Market Challenge'. Quite ahead of its time, this was a computer-based programme aimed at introducing the stock market experience to secondary school students. With the Stock Exchange office situated within an easy walk to a University, I grabbed the opportunity to complete my Masters' Degree in Education. Achieving this, coinciding with our youngest child leaving home, I began looking for a new challenge. A senior management position in a local, state-funded, co-educational secondary school became my new goal. After a few months of filling in application forms, pestering my colleagues to complete referral forms, and never making the short list, I realised it was time to re-evaluate my plans.

Determining that there must be something lacking in what I had to offer, interviews became opportunities to find out what my next step should be. From post-interview discussions it became apparent there was a perception that I lacked experience with teaching male students, especially those who exhibited problematic behaviours. Once this deficit was revealed, the solution appeared almost by magic.

Browsing through the senior management vacancies in the Ministry of Education's Gazette, I spied an advertisement for the head teacher/principal position of a school situated in a Youth Justice Residential facility catering for young violent offenders. Perfect. But frightening. Me? Teach young offenders? I closed the Gazette. Absolutely not! Days passed as I searched the papers for more suitable positions. But drawn to the Gazette and to the advertisement, I would read it over and over, as if there might be some subtle change in the wording. The niggling urge to go for the job grew but I continued to procrastinate. Should I apply? What were my chances of getting the position anyway? After all, I am New Zealand European, a middle aged female with little knowledge of working with 'antisocial' students let alone young offenders. The only thing I had going for me was that I'd worked my way up from the under-classes into the working classes, had some historical family connection with criminal behaviour, and had rubbed shoulders socially with people who offended as adolescents. I rationalised that I was also an effective teacher and surely that's what it was all about.

The day before the closing date, determining there was nothing to lose by 'throwing my hat into the ring', I rung and made an appointment to meet with the current principal of the Youth Justice Residential School. Before handing in my application, I wanted to visit the school to determine whether or not the position and I might be compatible. Given that the close of application date coincided with the interview, I filled in the form 'just in case'.

FIRST DAY AS PRINCIPAL

Most of my first morning at the Youth Justice residential school was taken up with my powhiri (Maori welcome) to the school. Following the traditional speeches and sharing of food, the guests left the school and I was left to observe the school staff, the residential social workers and the young people. The school staff consisted of one male teacher, one female teacher and a teachers' aide. The two teaching staff made it apparent from the outset that I was not welcome at the school in the role as principal. The teacher aide made it clear that I was very welcome. I came to admire, respect, and thank God for Janice.

The purpose of the school was to provide educational programmes for all the young people who had been ordered there by the courts. The two teachers, teachers' aide, and a roving cluster of anything from three to five residential 'social workers' supported the school staff. When I accepted the role of principal, it was my understanding that the social workers (whom the school personnel referred to as 'guards' when out of their hearing) were positioned in the school to ensure everyone's safety. It was their role to monitor and control the detained young people's behaviour.

That first afternoon can only be described as an afternoon from hell. Young people lounged around the open plan schoolroom and entered the kitchen, office and two small classrooms at will. The small room used as an art room contained a bench, small stained sink, running water and several unlocked cupboards that stored old paints and small 'bits and pieces'. The computer room contained three computers that had been loaded with *Doom* and other action 'kill-em-if-you-can' type games. It was a nightmare as the young people helped themselves to various items and roamed around banging on windows. I was told the residents often tested the shatter-proof security windows to see if they would break. The shelves that ran below the windows in the school contained hundreds of books. Pages were ripped out and paper darts flew above my head, the occasional one 'accidentally' connecting with various parts of my body. Some of the young people drew their 'tags' (graffiti names), not only in the books, but also on the walls and on the small desks that were scattered around the room. The atmosphere was nothing short of bedlam as the social workers tried to calm and contain the young people or sat alongside them and chatted as friends. Escorted by two large adult males, several boys were taken out of the school in head and arm locks, kicking and attempting to punch the walls and doors as they were removed. The noise that went with this action, along with the radio blaring in the background, added to the general pandemonium that was afternoon school.

Throughout the afternoon, the teacher aide rationed time for each student on the computers while the two teachers, clearly having developed an affinity with the residential staff, were sitting around chatting with the social workers and disengaged young people. At some point someone put on one of the few videos kept in the office. The young people gravitated towards the television and things appeared to settle into some kind of ordered routine. One of the teachers informed me that the video always settled them, it didn't matter that it was the same video day after day.

I don't remember what I was doing that afternoon, but I do recall feeling anxious and having a headache. While I believe that a new principal should take time to familiarise him or herself with the culture and organization of a school, my survival in the role as principal/head teacher at the Youth Justice Residential School was threatened if every day followed this same unstructured, chaotic pattern. I wondered how the staff and the young people coped day after day in such a negative, disorganised environment.

When the young people were led out of the school by the social workers at precisely 3 pm, I called an urgent, compulsory meeting with the school staff. The agenda of the meeting was to discuss what I had witnessed on this first day. From my perspective, the existing culture of the school appeared to be preceded by the term "a lack of ..." There was a lack of respect for the young people by the staff and a lack of respect for the staff by the young people. There was a lack of structure and routine appropriate to an institution with the title of school. There was a lack of purpose and a lack of a goal other than to survive the day. Afternoon school was a boring and stressful environment where no learning took place. I enquired if the morning programme was any different and was informed that some lessons were offered to those who wished to learn. One of the teachers smirked when I stated I would not last the week in such surroundings.

This first meeting was to set a new pattern for the school. Every day after the young people left we would have a 30 minute debriefing; the mornings would also begin with a 15 minute staff briefing prior to the young people being led into the school. School itself would begin with a 15 minutes forum where the young people would be divided up into three groups of five. Each group would rotate around the three teachers for formal lessons during the mornings. At this inaugural meeting with the staff, having ascertained the teaching strengths of the school personnel, it was determined that we would start with the basics. One teacher would specialise in teaching English, the other would teach social studies, and I would take mathematics. We were each to prepare a lesson that night, ready to introduce the next day. The teacher aide would continue to be responsible for the computers, providing regular, timetabled breaks from the formal lessons. Afternoons would be spent in 'options' such as board games, reading, drawing, suitable computer games and anything else that one of us could think up that would keep the young people positively occupied and engaged.

That evening, after everyone else went home, I checked what was on the school's computer hard-drives and deleted the games that focused on violence. This left one acceptable game, '*Need for Speed*', that involved racing cars. Turning to the principal's office, a search amongst the resources lying on the shelves and tucked away in cupboards revealed an unopened mathematics assessment pack. Yes! This treasure would give me an indication of what level each student might be on. Having specialised in commercial subjects, it also provided me with my first ever mathematics lesson. Using this invaluable resource, and through regular contact with the local Teachers Training College, I was later able to build on my very limited knowledge and develop individual education programmes in mathematics for the young people who came through the school. I spent the rest of that night planning how to implement positive change in the Youth Justice School. Setting my alarm clock, the 4 am starts to my day were reinstated.

THE SECOND DAY

Changing the way the school was managed began on Tuesday, my second day on the job. Rather than the social workers leading the young people into the school at 9 am, as was the norm, I explained to the supervisor, who was the senior social worker on the day shift, about the changes I wanted to introduce to the school routine. Instead of informing the young people of the changes within the confines of the school, I asked him if the school staff could meet with everyone together, the young people and the social workers, in the residential hall. This was a significant request as there was a clear demarcation between the school and residential side of the facility. While there was some initial resistance, the supervisor agreed to support the plan. This was very brave of him given we discussed the probability that the proposed changes would likely have a negative impact on their shift and his social workers. The young people did not respond well to change.

After outlining my ideas to the school staff, the four of us headed to the residential hall at the negotiated time. Following the formalities, which included a karakia (Maori prayer), at the supervisor's invitation I stood up and explained to the young people that the focus of the school was to be education rather than babysitting. I described how the mornings in school would look. We would begin with an assembly followed by 30-minute rostered periods taken up with formal lessons. Each lesson was to take the form of group learning. Groups of no more than five young people would be determined by me after the morning briefing with the night staff. The afternoons would be divided into two one-hour 'option' sections. Because there was a limit on resources such as computers, the option they could select for the afternoon would be based on their behaviour in the morning. I explained that during the last morning period their teachers and the teacher aide would be asked which students deserved to have the first choice of options. The best behaved would be given the first choice. There would be some restrictions. Under no circumstance could a young person elect to have computers across two options in one afternoon. Good behaviour in school was expected and would be rewarded. There was to be no unproductive loitering around the school arena, and both the school office and kitchen were out of bounds to all young people, at all times. Students had permission to be in the computer room or art room only if they were timetabled for lessons or options in these learning spaces.

The reaction to this speech was neither pleasant nor unexpected. When the moaning and expletives had quietened down, the young people were informed that a points system was to be put in place, with the 'points' being spent on Friday afternoon when we finished our week. A video would be hired from the local video shop and we would stock lollies, fizzy drinks, ice blocks and other edible 'goodies' that they could purchase with their points. The points system would start today. This got their interest and so I continued. Points would be awarded for effort, achievement and attitude. Each day, even on the worst possible day, some young person would be selected by the school staff as 'student of the day' and would be awarded a bonus of 50 points. One point would equal the value of 1 cent. Lollies would be sold on Friday afternoons commencing with bags valued at 50 points. No matter what the young person did, points earned could not be taken off them. However, any young person who committed a physical violent act against the school staff would not be eligible to attend school on the Friday afternoon of that week. Instead, they would spend that time in the residential facility under the supervision of a duty social worker.

The young people were invited to join us in the school under these new conditions. Their alternative choice was to stay in the residential hall accompanied by the social workers. I don't know who was more upset by that final statement, the young people or the social workers. The reaction was not promising. With another invitation to come to school under the new system, the school staff exited and returned to the school. No-one followed us and so we waited. What felt like hours later, a rather disgruntled supervisor entered the school and reported that none of the young people wanted to come to school under the new conditions. I told him we would continue to wait. He was not pleased and said they would bring them down anyway. I retaliated by threatening to close the school. I rung the deputy principal at the attached school and explained the position. She gave me her support, saying she would close the school down for the day if need be. At morning tea time the school personnel sat at a table, nibbling at biscuits and drinking hot tea without comment.

Mid-morning there was the sound of a key in the school's entrance door. A social worker entered, three young men behind him. "They are bored and want to come to school", he said. The sweetest words. By the end of the morning session we had a full contingent of students and social workers. The process of turning our school into an effective learning centre had begun. The new boundaries had been established but there was a long way to go.

SCHOOL VERSUS RESIDENTIAL STAFF

The relationship between the residential staff and me was never to be a comfortable one. This was indicated at the very first senior management meeting, attended by the residential manager, three senior supervisors, and myself. Someone made a negative comment, comparing my style of management and how the school was run under the direction of the previous principal. I mentioned my lengthy experience as a secondary school teacher, and reinforced this by revealing my newly acquired Masters of Education Degree. An audible gasp went around the room. It appeared that I had crossed some line by citing qualifications, and so with this statement I set myself apart from the others. From my perspective, this rift was never to heal. In my own defence, on reflection I doubt whether anything I could have done or said would have made any difference to this outcome. I was what I appeared to be – a white, working/middle class, middle aged, overweight female, and this was not the norm at the school (well the overweight part was okay). There was no point in my mentioning my own rise from the under-classes to the prestigious and desirable socio-economic label of school principal, although I did try to drop in dollops of my own familial history at times, but it all seemed so out of context, somehow verging, at best on self-pity, at worst a pitiful attempt to fit in. As I left the manager's office following that meeting, I felt very isolated. I did not belong here.

Two incidents occurred several months later that portray my relationship with the residential staff at the school. The first involved the death of my mother-in-law. Keeping with her wishes, mum's last days were spent at home, surrounded by her family and supported by the administrations of several wonderful nurses from the local Hospice. As she deteriorated, I wanted to be with my husband but also felt compelled to be at the school. I rarely took time off as it was almost impossible to get relieving staff and, given the policy ratio of one teacher to five students, the absence of a teacher meant some of the young people had to be kept out of school. The unlucky ones would spend their day in the residential hall, just sitting or filling in their time niggling at each other or playing with a ball.

Came the morning when our family realised that mum was unlikely to survive the day. Keeping with the school routine, I met with the residential night shift supervisor prior to the change-of-shift meeting. Sharing with him my distress and feelings of guilt regarding our current family situation, I warned that I might be called away and have to leave immediately, suggesting that we prepare a plan if this event were to occur. I also requested that, given I was feeling emotional and vulnerable, that his team be extra vigilant with the young people at the school. From experience I knew that if a staff member was having a 'bad' day, the young people sensed this and would react negatively, resulting in an escalation of incidences. I was mortified when the supervisor turned to me and suggested that I act like the professional I professed to be. He also said it was my role to put the job first. Humiliated and distraught, I left his office and made my way back to the sanctuary of the school office. When the door closed behind me, I burst into tears, my first at the Youth Justice School. When the school staff arrived we discussed the situation and agreed that I was not in an emotional state to run the school. Taking their advice I followed the established protocol, ringing my friend and mentor, the now acting principal at our affiliated secondary school. She instructed me to close the school immediately and to do nothing else until she got there other than to tell the morning supervisor to keep the young people on the residential side of the facility. There was considerable resistance to this and several unpleasant phone calls went between the supervisor and me. Appreciating the seriousness of the situation, I tried to contact the Youth Justice residential manager, but he was not on site and did not respond to the messages I left on his mobile phone.

As promised, my colleague arrived at the school. Her appearance was heralded by a thundering, "I am not that woman from the school, I am the Principal!" followed by the slamming of a door, then silence. I learnt later the supervisor had told the receptionist that he would not be available to meet with her when she arrived on site. He had other priorities. He underestimated this small-in-stature, huge-in-heart, formidable woman. Ten minutes later, she joined us in the schoolroom, listened to my report then sent me home on special leave. Mum died that evening. The following day, a large bouquet of flowers, and an apology, arrived at my home from the management and staff of the Youth Justice Residential Centre. From this incident I determined that the school staff could not rely on, and therefore needed to be independent of, the residential side. On my return to work, I announced that I would take full responsibility for what occurred when the young people were in the school, including the way that the young people were treated and handled by the residential staff. Outside the school doors, we had no jurisdiction. The division was set – it had become a 'them and us' situation. This lack of unity was reinforced with the second incident.

During my first six months at the school, when the young people left to eat their lunch in the residential dining room, Janice, the teacher aide, and I would eat our lunch in the main school room. Sometimes we opened the doors to let fresh air inside, but as we became accustomed to the oppressive lock-up experience, we would eat our food at one of the vacated tables. The other two teachers would take their lunch break in the residential staff room, but on rare occasions would eat with us in the school. On one such occasion we discussed our ethnic origins. Janice mentioned that she was part Maori. I shared that, whilst working on our family's genealogy for a University course, I had discovered that my paternal great grandmother was Jewish. We had been told our lineage was Italian so this came as a shock.

The next day was the last day of term. Always conscious of the young people's moods, I noticed that as the boys were led in, one young man, a staunch white supremacist and skinhead with Nazi swastikas tattooed on his scalp, was agitated. Usually friendly and respectful towards me, he kept glaring and scowling in my direction, muttering indecipherable comments. The other young people kept their distance from him but there was a general air of anxiety and apprehension. I put it down to being the last day of term. The young people had been complaining all week that the school holiday period meant two weeks of boredom. They described hours of sitting in the hall or working on programmes they did not enjoy. The school provided the comfort of routine.

The agitated youth was timetabled to have maths with me during the second period of the morning. He refused to come to the table but, coaxed by the social workers with threats of being removed from the school, he came over to our group, his bald head down, hands in his pockets. I opened up his maths folder and invited him to sit down next to me. Still standing, he put his hands on the back of a spare wooden chair then exploded. The chair and then the work on the table went flying across the room as he screamed "you filthy Jew, you fucking filthy whore."

I scrambled up from the table in shock. He dashed around the large, heavy wooden table I'd bought to replace the small desks, and chucked it onto its side. The other young people in my group sprang to their feet and took off across the room. Stunned, I just stood there whilst the young man continued to yell anti-Semitic abuse at me. He reached behind him and grabbed some encyclopaedias from the book shelves then hurled them at me as he spewed "we're gonna kill you all. You and all your filthy Jew kids and grandkids. You're all gonna be exterminated", spraying spittle as he ranted. I looked around the room, wondering why the social workers were not intervening. There were four in the room and they were all just standing there watching the performance. At first I imagined they were as shocked as I was by the sudden onslaught. Turning towards the two teachers who were standing at their respective desks I called out for support. Perhaps I was being oversensitive, but I could have sworn one of them sneered at me. When the disturbed young man reached out and grabbed at my upper arms the social workers mobilised and tackled him to the floor. He lay there exhausted but still muttering obscenities directed at me. The men hauled him onto his feet and dragged him out of the school. Everyone was quiet. Picking up the articles strewn around the room, I avoided looking at faces. Once the groups had settled back into their work, I left the school, my pulse still pounding in my chest, and wandered through the corridors until I reached the women's rest room. Shaking and nauseous, I retched into the hand basin. The bathroom door opened and a young relieving social worker walked in and put her arms around me. Being of Polynesian descent, she shared her own experiences of racial hatred and prejudices. This was my first real insight into what it must be like to belong to a minority group targeted by a society dominated by blind ignorance. I learnt never again to share my personal life with the two teachers who worked alongside me, or with any of the residential staff. It also left me with the feeling that I could not rely on the social workers to keep me safe in the volatile environment of a Youth Justice school.

Bruised and humiliated, the two weeks holiday was spent trying to recover from this experience. I feared the start of the new term. On the first day back after the holiday break, apprehensive, I greeted all the young people as they returned to the school. One of the last to come through the door was the young man who had attacked me. He did not look at me or respond to my greeting. Having earlier determined to get it over with as quickly as possible, I arranged for him to be in my first group of students. Without speaking, we sat together at the same large wooden table he had thrown to the floor. Concentrating on the other four students at my table, I left him alone as he worked on his maths problems. Realising he was having some difficulty I asked if I could help him. He said "yes" and we worked together, neither of us mentioning the earlier incident. Others told me he was remorseful, but I was wary of him. The following day he was released back into the community. I hoped no-one had given him my last name or home address.

POSITIVE CHANGE

By the end of my first term at the residential centre, the school had developed into a smooth and efficient learning environment. Rather than just marking time before they were released, the young people in our care were encouraged to focus on a variety of short-term academic goals, including unit standards, entry level external examinations, and passing the theory section of their drivers licence. Many left with what the school personnel, and even some of the residential staff, considered were very meaningful achievements.

At the end of my first year at the residential school, the two teachers who were there when I took up the position left us. One successfully applied for a year's study leave, the other teacher handed me his resignation in the final week of the term.

Believing that this specialised school would be closing the following year and that the young people remaining would be transferred to a purposely built, more secure youth justice residential facility, it was with some trepidation that I advertised two long term relieving teacher positions, anticipating few responses. I need not have worried however, as there were over a dozen applicants. The strongest candidate was a young Maori male but despite his initial expression of interest, he declined the position. Following several interviews, the position was offered to Peter, a reserved and gentle young man in his late twenties, recently arrived from the United Kingdom. Peter was both an experienced teacher and a commercial artist. The subjects he offered included English and art. The second teacher appointed was Smidy, a middle-aged gentleman of African-American descent. As well as an extroverted personality, Smidy brought with him impressive qualifications and practical experience as a scientist. He had only recently completed his training as a secondary school teacher and was looking for some practical teaching experience. Smidy offered the young people lessons in science, geography and life skills. He also brought a lot of fun and laughter into our school.

With the change in staff, the teacher aide's role was developed further to utilise Janice's strengths and rapport with the young people. As well as providing administration support and overseeing the computer room, Janice began teaching basic keyboarding skills. She was also timetabled to work alongside students with very limited literacy skills, using an approved remedial reading programme. In addition to managing the school, I continued to teach mathematics, word processing, computer literacy, and the social sciences.

It was with much enthusiasm that the school personnel opened the doors of our little school in my second year as principal. On that very first day it became apparent that the new mix of school personnel was perfect for the purpose of motivating the young people in our care. As we developed our goals and plans together, there was a feeling of unity that stayed with us as a team until the day the school closed. I am so grateful to Janice, Peter and Smidy for their wonderful work, their dedication, and acknowledge here the positive energy and enthusiasm they put into our school. As I share some of the stories where they were major players, it is always underpinned with the greatest respect and recognition of the excellent work that they did, not only for the young people, but also for me.

Our new, updated timetable offered English, science and mathematics after the school's morning assembly. This was followed by the social sciences, life skills and art courses which were offered three times a week, and Maori studies which was scheduled twice a week. As in the previous year, lessons in each subject were compulsory and were for periods of 30 to 35 minutes. We found that short periods were best for our young people, any longer and they not only lost concentration but sometimes found it difficult to begin. Our day almost always followed the same pattern. If we anticipated change to the routine of the school, I would go to the residential hall where the young people were gathered together, and inform them of the change before they came to school. By acknowledging the unexpected and pre-warning the young people of pending change, they were able to prepare themselves and adapt. This stopped reactive behaviour through unnecessary anxiety.

The usual morning routine was that up to fifteen young people would be escorted through the boys' wing and into the school area. On their entry into the school, they would go to a large post in the centre of the school where the day's groups would be listed. The groups would contain no more than five young people and would show the order of the subjects they would be taking that day. Each day there was a different grouping and, where possible the subjects would be offered in a different order from the day before. The young people would bring it to my attention if they had been given say, English (it didn't matter what the subject was), first up two days in a row. They were always listened to (copies of the previous days' list were always kept and used to avoid arguments) and where possible, their concerns were addressed. If the concern couldn't be addressed, the young person was withdrawn to the school's time-out space which was situated in the 'L' shape corridor between the school and the boys' wing. Once my own group of students were settled to their work and could be overseen by an attending social worker, I would join the complainant. We would sit on the floor together and try to find a suitable compromise. This process would give the young person time to feel listened to, calm down, accept that she or he would not be allowed to alter the structure of the group, and return to the school whilst still maintaining 'face'. The grouping was critical to how the school day would go and I learnt early on in my role as principal not to allow any young person (or social worker who would sometimes try and advocate for a young person) to manipulate the list. Predictable structure, fairness and honest, respectful communication were the key elements to our peaceful and productive school environment.

While the morning programme was always taken up with formal lessons, the afternoon programme for Monday through to Thursday was always electives, now broken up into two 50-minute periods. The electives being offered that day would be drawn up on a photocopied template which included five spaces on a computer for each period. The computers were popular as we now offered five modern computers and new challenging computer games. Because a period on the computers was sought after and there were only 10 opportunities each afternoon, initially no student was allowed to select two periods on the computers. An exception was later introduced where a student enrolled for an examination could book a second period for practice purpose. Examination preparation was always prioritised and became a popular option.

Establishing a process of selection that was acceptable to the young people was a challenge and required some flexibility. As the system developed, during the period before lunch, I approached not only the school personnel but also the residential staff, asking them to nominate students who had been working well that day. Once the information had been compiled, students nominated were invited to select their options first. This became an excellent behaviour management technique as the young people soon learnt that if they worked well in their lessons they got to choose first. Although the computers were very similar, because of licensing restrictions some of the computers had dedicated games that could not be played on another machine. To prevent students rushing into the room and fighting over the workstations, the computers were numbered. Those who got to choose first were able to select the computer, and the games, they favoured. Over the months, an interesting development appeared. Rather than the desirable computer games, several of the young people began to select 'supported study' for their electives as they prepared for examinations. We also began to notice a trend where the computers were used during elective and reward time for keyboarding and computer studies practice rather than for games. The desire to achieve and gain qualifications over entertainment was emerging.

Friday afternoons were always reserved for a rented video and the spending of acquired points. This time was very special to all of us, including the staff and the students. By the second year our points system had developed into an effective positive reinforcement strategy. Fifty points were offered to the 'student-of-the-day', determined by the school staff with recommendations often being made by the social workers on duty. We agreed that there would always be a 'student-of-the- day'. Even on a bad day, someone must be 'less bad' than the others. Occasions where two or more students were identified as worthy of the recognition became more and more frequent. There were also very rare times when all of the young people in the school were given the award. Every day when school finished with a five-minute assembly, the announcement of 'student-of-the-day' was made. The young people's interest in this positive form of respect never waned and it became the norm for other young people to congratulate the day's recipient as they were escorted out of the school. For many of the young people, good behaviour became a habit in the school and this normalised behaviour was passed on to new detainees. School personnel were always on the lookout for opportunities to reinforce acceptable behaviour. When a particularly difficult young person made an effort, this would be stated and the award given. Honest sharing of our observations and feelings of pride towards an individual became our norm.

I recall one young man, a known sexual offender, who was always scowling, rarking up the others and being sent out of school for profanities and verbal abuse. Refusing to participate in the education programme, tagging his books and worksheets, and niggling at the other students, there was just nothing nice about Johnny. Until one day someone pointed out that Johnny's behaviour was less offensive than on previous days. At the afternoon assembly, as the majority of young people waited for the desired announcement, to his astonishment Johnny was awarded 'student-of-the-day'. The reason given was that he had made an effort to be more pleasant in the school environment. Johnny's scowl was replaced by a surprised yelp of "fuck this," followed by the slightest tentative smile when everyone congratulated him. When he left the schoolroom he said goodbye to the teachers, a first for him. I would like to say that Johnny was fine after that, but he returned the next day even more offensive. Johnny hadn't changed, but our attitude changed towards him. Instead of over-reacting to his nastiness, the school staff would humour him out of his moods and occasionally he became the young man we felt was buried deep inside of him. On his last day at the school, Johnny approached each member of the school staff and shook our hands. Respecting their and our own personal space, we never hugged the young people. The only physical contact between us was a handshake and, when the occasion warranted it, a gentle pat on the shoulder. With some relief we all wished Johnny luck as he was released back into the community.

A NORMAL DAY

The makeup of the group was crucial to how the day would progress. Consideration had to be given as to which young people might work well together on that particular day. Ethnicity, gender, gang affiliation, who liked whom, what had happened overnight were all things that had to be taken into account. Each morning I would meet with the supervisor and the two cross-over teams from the night and day shifts. The social workers would highlight any incident that may have occurred and we would ascertain if there was a need to separate any young people. When there were more than 15 young people in residence, we would have to determine who would come to school and who would stay in the residential hall. If someone had an FGC (Family Group Conference) or court appearance, they would be the first to be selected to stay out of the school as they were often unsettled. This would also allow them reflection time. A young person who had just returned from court would also be considered, depending on his or her mood. Someone new to the residential centre would always be kept out of school so that I could meet with him or her individually, complete an academic assessment and be transitioned into the school via the afternoon programme. Any suspicions around a young person's attitude and/or behaviour would also be raised at these change-of-shift meetings, allowing us to watch for escalation in the school and to put preventative measures in place where appropriate.

All subjects were compulsory for all students, including Maori culture timetabled twice a week on Tuesday and Thursday mornings. Our affiliated secondary school allowed us to 'borrow' an enthusiastic and very gifted teacher for this role. Young people who were affiliated to the 'white supremacists' gangs would slouch in their seats, sullen and scowling, with a few sometimes participating in the singing. It was my hope that this brief immersion into the richness of the Maori culture would have a positive impact on these bigoted, ignorant young men. How could anyone not be moved by the young people's and staffs' voices joining together to raise the roof with their singing? I was often moved to tears on those mornings and thank this wonderful young man for what he contributed to our school experience.

Because of the security risk, the only open air the young people had access was at the rear of the complex. This was an enclosed small space surrounded by a high steel fence. There was another space squashed between the school, the boys' wing and the secure unit, but I don't recall ever seeing the young people out there. Perhaps it was used in the weekends or during the holiday periods when the school was closed? Fields surrounded the secure buildings and there were remnants of a concrete swimming pool we could see through the school windows. While we were forbidden to take the young people out for fear of them escaping, there were rare occasions when we were allowed to take them to the gym which was attached to the back of the residential section.

One such occasion was when we were able to offer lessons with the Tiaha. The Tiaha is a traditional Maori weapon used in close combat, a sharp-ended spear. While traditionally taught to males, our skilled, tolerant tutor allowed the girls and female staff to participate in the lessons. This was such a lot of fun and much appreciated. White supremacist youth were also encouraged to participate by our Maori tutor, however this often met with fierce resistance amongst the staunchest of young men. On rare occasions one or two shrugged off their bigotry, removed their socks and joined us on the floor.

We were always on the lookout for opportunities to enhance the young people's learning, but there appeared to be a general reluctance or fear in the wider community to work with our special students inside the school. Different groups would offer to meet with them off the Youth Justice campus but this was not possible because of the security risk. We did manage to find some outside providers, including experienced tradesmen, who would come in and teach a block course to those who were interested. Where appropriate, these tutors were invited to assess the students' proficiency and present them with evidence of their achievement, via computer generated certificates.

The young people were also encouraged to study for and sit external examinations extramurally. Given the short period they were to be at the school, we focused on opportunities that could be achieved and assessed in the short term and on our campus. Educational opportunities provided for the young people included: guitar lessons, a six-hour welding competency course, driver's licence – learners' theory, basic circuitry construction, the Primary Research Project, Practical English Certificate, Pitman's Keyboarding, Red Cross Certificate, Unit Standard 504 – 'Produce a Curriculum Vitae', the Asia Wise Competition, Pitman's English for Office skills, Pitman's Practical Word Processing, and Pitman's Commercial Numeracy. Much of the preparation for examinations and assessments occurred during the young people's election programme. Skills were also taught during the afternoon programme. Many of the young people made their own carved leather belt that they could take with them when they left the centre. Board games such as Chess, Stratego and Russian Backgammon were also encouraged. As girls began to increase in numbers, rug making was introduced. This also proved popular among some of the boys and the social workers. Two of the female social workers became adept at this skill and it was a delight to watch them working alongside the young people.

As the young people's behaviour improved in the school, it appeared that the residential social workers who were in the school solely for security purposes, became more and more bored. There were instances where the teaching staff suspected the residential staff were deliberately provoking the students. Several of the adults would sit on the chairs scattered around the room, talking and calling out derogatory remarks to the young people who were sitting at nearby tables. If a young person responded by swearing, giving the fingers or making some retaliatory remark, the social worker would spring to his feet, challenge the young person and a face-to-face confrontation would begin. Unless school staff or another social worker intervened, the inevitable result was the young person being taken out of the school accompanied by the social worker who had initiated the altercation.

After raising this as a concern at the management meeting, permission was given for social workers to work alongside the young people and support them in their learning. The role of the social workers in the school environment was transforming from guard to teacher aide. This change in role appeared to be appreciated by most of the female workers but was less welcome by some of the males. I recall one morning when you would have heard a pin drop as the young people concentrated on their lessons. One of the social workers, acting in the capacity as a relieving supervisor, walked into the school room and, banging the door closed behind him, yelled "fuck, school's boring!" Outraged, I jumped out of my seat and confronted him, demanding that he leave the school environment and return with a more respectful manner. I saw this as an opportunity to reinforce the atmosphere that we wanted in the school. Some of the young people laughed as the gentleman concerned backed out of the school. He did not return for several days, and when he did, his demeanour was respectful. This gentleman and I remained wary of each other but retained an air of politeness on the occasions when we did meet. This wariness escalated when, a few months later, I had the unpleasant task of reporting to the residential management committee that he was drawing gang signs on some of the students' artwork.

STORM

Storm was huge - a giant of a boy/man. Pencils clasped in my fist, the assessments tucked under my arm, I pushed open the doors of the residential hall and was confronted with the sight of an oversized, overweight adolescent dressed in black, loose fleece pants and a baggy black T-shirt. His back to me, standing on the wooden seat yelling obscenities at the social worker who was guarding him, Storm seemed to sense I was there and spun around. He stared at me, his face vacant. In a sudden, unexpected movement he jumped off the bench and challenged me. "Whatdyawant bitch?"

I introduced myself, extending my right hand towards him in an invitation to shake and invited him to join us in the school.

He ignored the hand. "Ain't goin to no fucking school, I ain't no fucking kid!" he bellowed. "I got me own fucking kids, bitch!" he roared. "I'm a man." "I got me a fucking woman at home so fuck off*!" And with that he jumped up onto the bench, turned away from me and swung his bare foot back and forth. Seconds passed in silence. "Shit." he yelled, spinning around to face me, "and who made you the fucking boss of me?" "I ain't going to no fucking school."

"Okay" I said, "but seeing that I'm here anyway, how about you help me with the paperwork"?

"Nah" he grunted, "ain't goin to no fucking school like no kid and ain't doing no test neither."

Oh great, I thought to myself. "Okay, how about I just sit here and keep you company for a while".

"Nah, fuck off" he said, waving his hands in dismissal and punching his middle finger into the air.

The social worker grinned. "Guess you ain't going to get this one," he jeered. There was no love lost between me and this man and I glared at him. Turning to the new resident, I stated "I'll be back this afternoon. In the meantime, you can send for me if you change your mind".

They laughed together. With as much dignity as I could muster, I left them to it. After lunch one of the other social workers came into the school and said Storm wanted to see me. Once the school was settled, I returned to the hall and approached the young man slouched on the bench. "Hi Storm, you sent for me?"

He looked up, his dull gaze focusing behind me. "Yeah, I'll come to your fucking school but I ain't doin no fucking kid's school work."

"Okay" I responded. "But first you need to do an assessment for me."

"Fuck that" he spat, starting to rile up. "Let's go".

"Nope, assessment first," I insisted.

"No shit!" he roared. "Told ya, I ain't doin no test." I just stood there, saying nothing until he quietened down. "Why test?" he asked.

"Everyone who comes into the school does an assessment," I explained, with what I hoped was a calming smile on my face. It's how I know what work to give you. If the work's too easy you get bored and think I think you're dumb. If it's too hard you get embarrassed and it makes you angry. This test helps all the teachers give you work at a level that is right for you."

"I can't write well", he muttered, dropping his head into his hands. "My girlfriend reads for me".

"No problem, I said. "We'll do it together". With that we sat down on the wooden bench and worked through the assessment tasks. It turned out that not only was Storm illiterate, he also struggled to write, the pencil held at an awkward angle in his oversized fist. At least he knows his alphabet, I thought as I spelt out each word for him and watched him struggle with the pencil.

Within hours of Storm being in the school the teachers realized he was 'challenged'. Storm just couldn't get it. I started him off on level one math and had to simplify the tasks using imagery and colour pegs. Peter tried to introduce sequencing skills supported by colourful cue cards. We tried to get a 'buddy' to write to Storm's dictation, but nothing seemed to 'stick'. We tried varying his lessons but soon accepted that Storm was happiest with repetition. He enjoyed mastering the same task over and over again. Storm was also obsessed with trucks and so I purchased a child's book about trucks that had a few words and lots of colourful pictures. He pored over the book, asking the school staff, social workers, and some of the friends he made in the unit to read it to him, over and over again. You'd expect that he would know the words off by heart, but he never read the words out loud and never tired of hearing someone read this simple little book to him. The day he left the school we gave him the truck book, but he threw it on the table and said he didn't want it. "Got no need for it now" he said. "Hate books; hate baby books. Don't need no books at home. Got me a woman."

This was Storm's other obsession – his girlfriend. He talked about her over and over again. According to Storm, she was beautiful, gorgeous. They had two little boys together and he wanted lots more babies with her. I cringed but kept silent. He was only sixteen years old. He had no job, no skills, they were living on a government benefit and he was committing crimes. And he wanted more babies? I guessed that making babies was something Storm could do. Something he did well and something he could be proud of.

Storm's girlfriend's name was Celeste and we were fed stories about her beauty, her talents, what a great mum she was, how all his mates wanted her. He left nothing to the imagination. By now everyone had come to appreciate that our very large man-boy struggled in the intellectual department. Some of the boys would cruelly tease him about his precious Celeste. Unable to control his emotions Storm would sob his heart out, much to their pleasure.

Then came the day when Storm bounced into the school. He was so excited; over the moon with happiness. His Celeste was coming and she was bringing his boys to see him. His lawyer had arranged a family visit. Storm jumped and whooped around the school, he just couldn't wait. They would be allowed to spend the afternoon together in the residential facility whare (Maori meeting house). He was so excited he kept spinning around the school room, banging into tables as he worked out on his fingers how many sleeps before they came.

The family visited on a Tuesday. Storm came into the school just for the morning. He had showered, washed his hair and was dressed in some fresh clean clothes, including new white socks. He was all smiles, and for Storm, subdued. His anticipation was contagious and there was an air of expectation and curiosity, as we all wanted to catch a glimpse of the beautiful Celeste. Just before lunch, a taxi drove onto the property. Storm, accompanied by most of the other young people (and one or two staff members) rushed to the window. The taxi stopped outside the residential front entrance. Because of the angle we couldn't quite make out the person stepping out of the taxi. Was it her? The tension mounted in the room and Storm became more agitated as he paced by the school office. Minutes passed before a social worker came to the school door and beckoned for Storm. This was it. He beamed at everyone, waved and exited. Everyone's eyes were glued to the window. The whare was situated across from the school and Storm and his family would have to pass us to get there. Then we saw them. There was stunned silence. Accompanied by two residential social workers, a little boy hanging on his hand, Storm walked beside a woman carrying a baby. Celeste? That couldn't be the beautiful Celeste? This woman was old enough to be his mother. A titter went around the school room. There's no nice way to say this; she was a very unattractive woman. Short, emaciated, her long, thin, straggly hair did little to hide the bulging eyes, scabby skin and fleshy nose. A grinning Storm pointed at the window and Celeste waved and smiled broadly, revealing black gaps amongst misshapen teeth.

Storm disappeared into the whare with his family. The next morning a very subdued and unhappy Storm was led into the school, along with the other young people. Refusing to leave the assembly area, his eyes downcast, and hands dangling between his knees, Storm sat on one of the seats, hunched over and crying. One of the female social workers sat beside him and put her arm around his shoulders. She told me later that the other boys had given Storm a hard time about his girlfriend. They had called her a dog and laughed at him. I never heard Storm talk about Celeste again after that, or about his children. Sometimes I hated the hardened insensitivity and the deliberate cruelty of the young people in my care.

THE GANG CULTURE

The gang culture in the Youth Justice facility, like the tags and other graffiti, was everywhere throughout the residence. My first awareness of the different gangs the young people were affiliated to came via compliments on my clothes. On days when I wore blue, one group would tell me how good I was looking that day, while others would scowl and become non-compliant. On another day I wore red and a similar response occurred when they walked in, "Hey miss, you're looking cool today," and I'd get the thumbs up from another group. After a few days of this I twigged. The Mongrel Mob youth liked the red while the Black Power young people responded with praise to the blue. This was addressed during the morning forum when it was made clear to all the young people, and staff, that my choice of clothing would not be influenced by their prejudices. They were informed that the school was to be a 'gang-free neutral zone' for the period of their internment. I was surprised that this worked, but it did as I stopped receiving compliments regarding my attire and the drawing of tags became more discreet within the school environment.

Tagging was always a problem in the school. It was like the young people took ownership of the place by putting their graffiti names on anything they could reach. It never ceased to amaze me that, despite the surveillance of residential and school staff, tags would appear in the most unlikely places at incongruous times. For example, on the ceiling, in the middle of the morning, in an open space where there was nothing for a person to stand on or get leverage to reach up to the high ceiling. Wouldn't we have noticed them jump? And what were they writing with? We took considerable care to count all the pencils that were given out. Felts and pens were never distributed to the young people. Art was always with water-based paint, coloured pencils and pastels. No young person was allowed to leave the school for any reason (including going to the toilet) unless we had first counted out the pencils, rulers and rubbers. We were scrupulous in this because experience had shown how easily these items could be turned into weapons, used as a means of escaping, or even worse from our perspective, provide an opportunity for residential staff to blame school staff for negligence. Unless the count was correct, the young people could not be taken out of the school for their morning tea or lunch.

I recall one afternoon when the count was correct but it was evident that one of the pencils had been snapped in half – there remained a whole pencil out there! All the young people were seated in the assembly area, ready to be escorted out. Each denied knowledge of the missing pencil. We all waited. Nothing. One of the techniques we used was to invite everyone to search the school. During the search someone would 'find' the missing pencil, but not this day. We searched and searched. Again, nothing. Someone suggested that the two halves were in fact two pencils. I checked with the teaching staff. It was definitely two halves.

An hour passed and it was getting very unpleasant. Several of the morning staff had opted to stay on until this crisis was over. The afternoon shift was on now and they wanted the young people out in the residential side as they had planned a special activity. We couldn't let them go - this was to be our "high noon". This was more than a missing pencil. It was a challenge, but it was also an opportunity to reinforce the rules and show our strength. Some of the young men began pacing the school. The mood had become threatening and, despite the presence of residential staff, I found myself cornered by three boys demanding they be released.

Pressure was also mounting from the adults and it was beginning to look as if we had painted ourselves into a corner. The afternoon supervisor and I began to strategise as to how we could cancel this standoff without losing face. I was leaning towards collective accountability that would require a group consequence, but was loath to do this. It was probable that the consequence would be the cancelling of our Friday afternoon video. The young people and the staff always enjoyed and looked forward to Friday afternoons. The reaction to this consequence would be unpleasant. With no way out, I shared this dilemma with the young people. As I was talking, one young man waved his hand and said he needed to go to the toilet. It was urgent. Others joined in, saying they needed to go too. Legally and ethically such a request could not be refused. The afternoon supervisor agreed to escort them to the toilet. Those who wanted to go to the bathroom lined up in single file. As they shuffled off through the narrow corridor into the school, someone called out, "Hey, there it is!" Between their collective feet lay a discarded red pencil, its lead sharpened to a long point. No one took responsibility for how it got there, and no one cared. With an audible sigh of relief, all the young people and supervising adults left the school.

We never again had to stay in after school looking for a missing pencil. Of course, pencils and other bits and pieces went missing, but they usually appeared within minutes of an announcement being made. Phew. That night I went home and poured myself a stiff gin and tonic. It would not be my last.

VIOLENT YOUNG OFFENDERS

Sometime during my second year working with the young offenders, at a time when the school was settled and the students were making progress, I was confronted by another violent young man. Unlike the incident with the skinhead youth, this incident did not appear to be personally or racially motivated. Sean was just a young person who grasped every opportunity to lash out and hurt someone. Although there were occasions when he displayed physical aggression, the facility was filled with violent young offenders and Sean didn't stand out as being a greater risk than anyone else. On the day he confronted me, I was standing between the math table and a low bookcase that was nailed to the wall. Above the bookcase were windows that overlooked the secure unit. A female resident was sitting at the table and, whilst maintaining a respectful distance, I was leaning over her, explaining how to work out a math problem. Sensing a movement close behind me I straightened up. As I turned a fist grazed the side of my head and connected with the top of my ear. The strike was accompanied with expletives and a peculiar smile. While shocked I realised if Sean had wanted to hurt me, his fist would have connected with my head. I decided that he was just playing a perverse game and asked the attending social workers to remove him from the school for the rest of the day. Laughing, Sean offered no resistance when they escorted him away.

The next day, along with the other young people Sean was led into the school at the usual time. By midmorning he had commenced a new cat-and-mouse game with me. His technique was to get behind me and whisper inane threats that were beyond the hearing of anyone else. I worked at keeping him in sight and at a distance. He would smile as each little move met with a counter move. I ignored him. Losing interest in this game, Sean became frustrated and his manner developed more sinister tones. His whispered voice became louder and the comments more intimidating. I asked that he be removed to time-out so that we could talk it through, hoping to defuse the situation before it escalated to something more sinister. A relieving social worker, a male who was on a two week trial, accompanied us to the boys' wing. He stood close by as I asked Sean what was going on. From Sean's response I concluded that it was his intention to do me some physical harm. Leaving Sean under the care of the attending social worker, I left the boys' wing and sought out the shift supervisor. In his office I shared my concerns, requesting that Sean be kept out of school for the rest of the day. The supervisor dismissed my fears, explaining that being threatened was a risk we took in this line of work. As Sean had done me no real harm he would not be removed.

Returning to the school required me to walk back through the boys' wing. By now it was the lunch break and the young people were milling around the boys' wing corridor, waiting to be taken into the dining room. I scanned their faces and noted that Sean was not amongst them. Walking through the gauntlet of young people I sensed his presence, but it was too late. Passing the door leading to the boys' toilet, Sean jumped out and with a loud, high pitch scream, he screeched into my left ear. The pain was excruciating. As I reeled from the attack I spotted a nearby man laughing. It was the relieving social worker who had accompanied us to the boys' wing earlier. With my hands holding my head, I staggered back to the school. This incident resulted in my being off work on sick leave for several days with a burst eardrum. When I reported the incident to the residential management staff, an investigation was carried out. The outcome was a note from the relieving social worker who said he thought it was all just a bit of fun. Both the relieving social worker and Sean were kept out of the school for a few days. On those occasions when our paths crossed, the young man would smile and say "Boo!" or, giggling, ask how my head was. One of my happiest moments at the Youth Justice School was being told that Sean had been shifted to another site during the night.

It was common to find that a young person had been moved to another youth facility at an hour or two's notice. We would close their education file and store it in the school office, anticipating the likelihood that the young person would return. If they returned, the file would be opened and the work continued where they left off. As I closed Sean's file, I muttered a secret prayer that he would never return.

A follow-up to this story occurred a short time later, at our morning assembly. It was a day when the relieving social worker was on duty in the schoolroom. As was our normal practice, everyone was invited to greet the group in any language that they related to, other than English. To support the process, samples of various greetings were written in large letters all around the room. After the greeting each person was entitled to speak to the assembled group about their concerns or thoughts. In this way we were often able to ascertain the mood of the group and talk through any matter that might be unsettling them. Out of courtesy, after the young people had spoken, the social workers were encouraged to say something if they wished. When invited to participate, this particular reliever stood to attention, clicked his heels, raised his hand palm outward and greeted us with "Sieg Heil!" much to the amusement of the two white supremacists in the group. The two boys jumped to their feet, yelling with excitement. This spectacle was not to be tolerated and I confronted him over it. He became antagonistic and, frothing at the mouth, insisted on his right to use the Nazi greeting, claiming German heritage. I demanded he leave the school which he did, giving me the fingers as he departed. I asked the two boys if they wanted to leave but they opted to stay and settled down. The day continued without further incident. I never again had to tolerate this unpleasant gentleman, as I was told later that day his services were no longer needed at the residence. This particular incident served a useful purpose. It reinforced to the young people present that even residential staff were expected to follow the rules of the school.

SCHOOL SECURITY

Given that almost all of the young people at the Youth Justice residential facility were categorised as serious, violent and, in many cases, repeat offenders, we were always conscious of security in the school. My first and final duty of the day was to check all the school doors were locked. There were three entrances into the school, one through the boys' wing, another via an outside door that opened into the 'time-out' space in the school's 'L' shape corridor, and a third door that was situated at the end of the school. This third entrance overlooked the Youth Justice Residential Centre's whare and opened onto a road outside the grounds. The windows in the school were never opened and almost all the windows had been replaced at some time with non-breakable glass. We would often see a new resident tapping on the glass to ascertain its vulnerability, or trying the door handles to see if some absentminded person had forgotten to lock up. This did occur on occasion, when the school staff started to relax around the young people. The entrances became a bone of contention between the school and residential staff with social workers checking the doors every hour. We were amused by seeing the staff and the young people sneaking around, trying not to be observed as they tested out the door handles, looking for escape opportunities.

For various reasons, usually because of aggressive acts, young people were separated from the others and locked away in a 'secure' part of the residence. One of my morning responsibilities was to put together an educational programme for any young person confined to the secure unit. While I never kept records of when and who was in the secure unit, it became obvious during my second year at the Centre that less young people were taken out of school because of problematic behaviours and my visits to the unit became less frequent. Several social workers reported to me that the young people hated missing school and so they deferred their 'acting out' for the weekends and school holiday periods. While this was stated with some criticism alluding to what was perceived as the teachers' excessive school holidays, I was delighted, as these comments provided evidence that our young people valued what the school was offering.

Keys were always a problem in the school. There was a master key for moving around the residential centre, and individual keys for specialised areas such as the school, the office and the secure wing. My keys were bunched up on a small key ring and kept in the pocket of my trousers, skirt or jacket. One day I realised to my horror that my keys were missing. Too embarrassed to tell anyone, I searched high and low to no avail. Then the time came for the young people to be escorted out of the room for their midday meal. At this point I had to own up that I had 'misplaced' my keys. The young people were kept back from lunch, as we could not release them until the missing keys turned up. By keeping the students contained in the school area, we knew that the keys were localised; by releasing them to the residence, there would be a greater area to search if the keys did not materialise. After ten minutes, no doubt his stomach telling him he was missing lunch, one young man put his hand in his pocket and handed me the missing keys. With much embarrassment and apologies to the young people and the social workers, I returned the keys to my pocket. For the rest of the afternoon, I kept patting my pocket to reassure myself they were still there. After work I purchased a solid silver bangle and a strong latched hook. From then on I always wore the bangle on my left wrist with the keys securely attached and visible.

Another incident around keys meant that we had to revisit the whole process of how school staff managed security issues. A relieving teacher was given the necessary keys to enter and leave the school. One day he became so engrossed in his demonstration of how an electrical circuit board functioned, he handed his keys to a young person to hold whilst he struggled with a loose piece of wire. There was a stunned silence, a moment in time when everyone in the room appeared to freeze. The boy couldn't believe it. Spotting the event from across the room, nor could I! I think one of the social workers and I flew at that young boy so fast, he wondered what had hit him. He dropped the keys in shock and they were in my hand before they hit the floor. This incident illustrates just how aware we all were of what was happening in other parts of the open plan schoolroom. After that day, it became school policy that keys were not to be given to relieving teachers. Instead they were expected to knock on doors to be let in and out.

Despite all our precautions, we had two escapes from the school. The first involved Smidy. Smidy was a popular teacher with a relaxed style of teaching that encouraged learning. He treated all the young people with courtesy and respect, even those who were disparaging about the colour of his skin and his accent. Inexperienced with young offenders, Smidy was relaxed in the way that he interacted with our young people, a number of whom were cunning and smooth-tongued. Smidy took all the young people at face value and, despite a number of cautions he trusted and allowed different individuals more and more leniency. For a brief period we decided to trial cooking lessons. Smidy took a group into the kitchen with the purpose of teaching them to cook for themselves and others. This was a risky task given the potential alternative uses for common utensils found in the kitchen. But Smidy was vigilant, and all knives, forks, etcetera were always accounted for.

During one cooking period, Smidy noted that they were short of some crucial ingredients. He determined that these ingredients might be acquired from the residential kitchen. Taking two young people with him that he trusted, Smidy walked out of the school complex, through the boys' wing, across the main corridor, through the communal dining room and into the kitchen. He later explained that the two boys who accompanied him stood behind him as he approached one of the kitchen-hands and explained their culinary needs. Together, the two adults stepped into the large walk-in pantry, leaving the boys waiting, compliant and respectful, in the kitchen area. It was not until they emerged a few minutes' later, Smidy's arms laden with the necessary ingredients, that he realised the two boys were not where he had left them. An unlocked exit door off the kitchen that led to the rubbish bins, and the great outside world, was ajar. The boys had seized their opportunity. A mortified and distressed Smidy was obliged to report that he had 'lost' two of the residents. Several days later, the 'escapees' were returned to the residential facility, but Smidy's trust in the young people was damaged and he never returned to his original level of naivety.

It was this incident that gave me an awareness of the vulnerability of the employees of institutions similar to the Youth Justice residential centre. As part of the security, we always went by our first names, although for some reason I was always referred to as "Miss", not only by the young people, but also by many of the residential staff. Our last names were never used in front of the young people, although I was required to sign off formal documents with my full name, which rather defeated the purpose of first name labelling. When the two missing boys returned to our school, one shared how much the school next to my home had changed. Puzzled, I asked him what he meant. He explained that he had once attended the college that I lived next door to and that he had called in to visit me whilst he was free but I wasn't home. He confided that he had leaned against my fence and watched as a prefab building was transported from the college campus. When I questioned how he knew where I lived, he said everyone knew my last name and my address was in the phone book. I found this all rather disconcerting and became a trifle paranoid if I suspected anyone was hanging around outside my front gate. I rung Telecom and asked that my name, address and phone number be removed from the next telephone directory. By the time this was actioned, the Youth Justice School had closed and the young people and I had moved on.

The second 'great escape' resulted in us losing our only constant source of fresh air into the school. Peter was an artist as well as the English teacher so we converted the little room opposite the computer room into an art studio. Art was a compulsory subject for all young people three times a week but was also offered as an elective in the afternoons. Several boys were very creative and grabbed at these extra opportunities to work in the art studio. Two boys in particular bonded with Peter and took some ownership of this space. Always mindful that some of our residents were substance 'sniffers' and would be attracted to fumes and emissions, we had removed all acrylic paints and only stocked water based paints, as well as chalk, crayons, pencils and pastels. Because of the closeness of the space and the tendency for this room to overheat, two small fanlights above the benches were kept open about two inches to allow for air movement. For security reasons they were screwed into place.

Sometimes Peter found working for long periods in this small space a bit of a trial, particularly on a hot day. Despite residential staffs' efforts to keep the young people clean, the boys' hygiene was not always as it should be and close proximity to them could be rather challenging. Sometimes, when he felt the budding young artists were not in need of his full attention, Peter would grab an opportunity to stand in the doorway, one eye on his charges, every so often chatting to other members of staff or a young person. The escape incident happened within a space of a few seconds. I was in the school office, across from the art studio, Janice was in the computer room with a group of students and Smidy was in the main schoolroom with another group. I don't recall where the social workers were. There was a sudden bang! Peter yelled. I jumped out of my seat and within two strides was at Peter's side. He was standing in the doorway, his mouth open, pointing up towards the art studio fanlight windows. Looking across his outstretched arm, I saw the shape of two of our boys running for their lives down the driveway. The one closest to us was hopping along on one foot; he had lost a sock. While running and hopping, he was trying to pull his trousers up onto his hips. The fugitives sprung over the fence and then they were gone from sight. Peter tried to tell me that the boys had escaped; I could see that for myself. All I could think was "Oh my Lord, not another escape from the school". Peter explained that he'd been distracted by two boys who began an argument with him. On investigation we found that it had all been prearranged. The screws in the Art room's two fanlights had been loosened over preceding days. At a signal from one of their mates the two boys jumped up onto the bench, flicked the loosened screws holding the fanlights ajar, and wriggled through the gap. The second boy's trousers had become stuck and were around his knees by the time he fell to the ground. It was with a sinking stomach that I rung the Residential Manager's office to report the second escape from the school in as many months. Later that week, we would learn that numerous screws were missing on the security windows attached to the boys' wing. Some of the windows were held together with two screws rather than the twelve required. One mighty boot to each window and there could have been a mass escape. But at least it wouldn't have been from the school.

"I AIN"T GOING TO NO SCHOOL!"

The atmosphere moved from calmed focus straight into pandemonium as young people rushed to the south easterly-facing windows and clambered onto the bookshelves and windowsills. Once at the windows, they did an excellent imitation of apes, jumping, pawing at the glass giving abusive signs and shouting profanities. "Pigs! Fucking pigs, PIGS*!" they screeched. Even the so-called 'cool' young people were part of the agitated mob. Without fail, the arrival of a police car or a uniformed police officer evoked this response. Resigned to the school's routine being disrupted, I wandered over to the back windows that overlooked the entrance to the secure unit. "Oh no", I groaned as I recognised the boy sitting in the back seat of the police car. It was our 'refuser'. They were bringing him back for his third stint at the Youth Justice facility. The 'refuser' was so-named because he would refuse to come to school, refuse to do any of the school's assessments, and refuse to attempt any work. Faced with his obstinacy over days, we conceded defeat and tried bringing him into the school without an initial learning assessment. On his first visit he lasted for less than half an hour before acting out and being dragged off by the attending social workers to spend the remainder of his stay in the secure unit. Because of his small size, the school staff nicknamed the refuser, 'Peewee'. Peewee's 'acting out' was pretty amazing to observe – he'd fly around the room, bounce off the walls in his bare feet, spring up to the ceiling and scatter everything that wasn't nailed down, including books, paintings, games, and posters. On a good day he would manage to shred at least two books before they could overpower and remove him, spitting and screeching, from the school. When I visited him in the secure unit, Peewee would refuse to acknowledge my presence, ignored my questions and never bothered with the work or activities that I tried to tempt him with. Now Peewee was back for the third time. Given our history, I wondered how long he'd give us before he performed his usual tricks to get himself locked into the familiar safety of the secure unit. Why anyone would prefer to be locked up in the security wing, I had no idea. The bedrooms off a small open space were miniature cells and there was very little privacy, even for toileting. The young people were locked in there, hour after hour, day after day, under constant supervision. It became quite distressing not only for them, but also for those in the school situated directly across from the unit. Sometimes the confined young people would go 'stir-crazy' and we'd hear them banging on the walls, yelling and screaming at the top of their voices. Peewee was one of the loudest and now he was back.

Given that everything else we tried had failed, the school staff agreed it was time for a different tactic. Granting Peewee the customary day to settle down, the next morning I approached him as he sat on the hard bench in the hall, watching television. "I ain't going to no fuckin' school" he yelled at the TV screen. "Okay", I said as I sat down next to him. Together we watched the cartoons for a few minutes, then, still focusing on the TV programme, I asked if he would like to try the assessments this time, or should we just change the rules again and he come into the school in the afternoons and play some of the computer games. Expecting the usual impulsive outburst of verbal abuse, I was surprised when he responded with a grunted "yeah". Not wanting to push him any further, and before he changed his mind, I moved off the couch and walked away, wondering if we would see him in the school that afternoon.

The residential staff returned the young people to the school after lunch and there was little Peewee, last in line. One could sense that he was wound up like a tense spring, and as I approached him he became jittery, his eyes flittered around the school. Perhaps Peewee suspected a trap? "You're on number three computer", I told him. "It's set up with a racing car game". He darted off into the computer room where Janice was waiting, ready to set him up so there'd be no glitch and no frustration to escalate his anxiety level. Against our own rules, we allowed Peewee to stay on the computer game until school was over. I expected the other young people to complain, but no one did, even when Peewee stayed at the computer when the others went to the afternoon closing assembly. When school was over, we had to turn the computer off so Peewee would move out of the chair. "You can have it tomorrow afternoon", we told him. "See you in the morning". I had my fingers crossed behind my back.

The next morning Peewee arrived with the group. To my surprise he followed the others and sat on the couch during the welcoming assembly. Then it was time for the first lesson. Peewee was timetabled to begin at the math table with me. As he had never attempted any of the numeracy assessments, I decided to assume he had no knowledge of numbers and so offered him several easy tasks. He sat at the maths table with the others in his group, picked up the folder with his name on it, flicked open the cover and checked out the worksheets. He then grabbed the pencil offered to him and flew through the tasks. I grabbed some spare sheets that were at a higher level and he flew through most of these as well, leaving out the problems that involved words, coping well with the problems involving numbers. Watching him as I worked with the others at our table, I wondered if Peewee couldn't read. It was time to change subjects and his next lesson was English. Peewee refused to go to the English table. Not a problem. After a quiet word with Peter, I invited Peewee to stay at the maths table and that's where he stayed all morning, doing page after page of number problems. This was the longest Peewee had stayed in the school with no hint of a behaviour melt down. That afternoon, as promised, Peewee played his racing game on the computer and no one complained that he was receiving preferential treatment. This time Peewee joined us at the closing assembly.

The following morning, before school commenced and while the other young people were engaged in their various clean-up activities, I invited Peewee for a private chat. He was very obliging and followed me into a small office where there was a very large, soft cushion on the floor. He nestled into the cushion and I sat beside him on the hard ground. We talked about the computer games he liked. He suggested I buy some more. We talked about his maths. He told me he liked numbers. Our conversation moved towards books. Peewee hated books. He hated books because they make him feel dumb. Kids thicker than him could read and he couldn't read and that was stupid. From this talk I discovered that Peewee wanted to be able to read but he couldn't lose face by trying and failing. He told me he would not try to read in front of the other young people. He explained that he was a gang prospect and needed to be 'tough'. I think he meant 'respected'. Peewee was ashamed and embarrassed that he couldn't read and confused many of the common letters. He told me he had never been enrolled at school; he didn't recollect ever attending a school. He was raised in a 'gang house' and spent most of his time with the dogs.

Peewee was like a little bedraggled canine himself. His mannerisms, the way he'd crouch and the way he would tilt his head when he was listening reminded me of a dog. He also had a way of sniffing the air that resembled a feral animal checking for danger. And so together we hatched a plot where no one else would know he was having remedial reading lessons. Every day I would have to find some fault with him (he was quite happy to oblige with incidents to support this part of the plan) and send him to time-out in the boys' wing. I was then to follow him but instead of punishment, we would have our lesson, which began with phonetics. This repetitive sounding out of the alphabet was supported by picture words that were relevant to his life world. For example, the letter 'p' was accompanied by pictures of police and pig. For over a week we did this. Peewee would perform some trivial act of non-compliance and I'd send him out and follow him armed with work sheets and word cards. We'd study together, kneeling on the floor or the boys' sofa, head to head playing with the cards, with Peewee always keeping one eye on the school door. If he saw someone coming he'd grunt and I'd start the agreed lecture about him having to behave in school. When the approaching person had passed by, we'd continue with the lesson. This facade ended when two boys approached me with the complaint that I was being too hard on Peewee. They said they didn't think it was right that I was always picking on the kid because he couldn't read. The young people had always known that Peewee couldn't read – it was our huge secret that wasn't a secret to them.

All pretence now evaporated. Everyone, including the young people, the social workers and even the dining room staff, encouraged Peewee to sound out syllables and words. He became a bit of a celebrity and I suspect that he rather enjoyed all the attention. We would all smile at him and tell him how clever he was. He still continued to run and bounce around the school, but now it was from poster to colourful poster, tapping the picture and sounding out the different words. He made rapid progress in his reading. One morning, with no warning, Peewee was gone. The collaborative environment that had developed between the young people and all the staff, fostered through the common desire to support this bright, likeable young man, disappeared with Peewee. For a few days we grieved for his loss. When I enquired after Peewee I was informed he had been transferred to another Youth Justice Residence. I never could fathom why they took Peewee away from us when he was doing so well. Peewee never returned to our school. I still wonder what became of this vibrant and special young man.

THE GIRLS

The average length of time the girls attended the school was 17 school days. 'School days' refer to the actual number of days the young people attended the school, and excludes weekends, holiday periods and the days they were out of school, either because they were in the secure unit, on leave, at Court or attending a Family Group Conference. This was less than the boys who tended to be at the school for longer periods.

Given the smaller number of girls coming through the school, there were periods of time when we operated as a 'single-sex', 'boys-only' environment. We came to appreciate these times, as they were more peaceful, without the distractions created by the surge and clash of adolescent hormones. Enter one girl into the school and the peace was broken. The first few days after a girl arrived were always challenging. The focus of the majority of the boys centred on this girl as they vied for her attention. Many of our young people were socially inept. Unable to communicate with the girl in what might be considered a more appropriate way, they would draw attention to themselves by being loud, using obscene language and showing off various parts of their body. A shirt would be raised to show a hairless chest, sleeves drawn up to display tattoos. They became non-compliant and argumentative with staff and each other. Some of the boys would make personal comments about the girl's appearance or gender. During the lessons they would vie for her attention by grabbing, vandalising or tagging her work. This behaviour would stop once the girl indicated she favoured one boy. Peace reigned when it was announced that the new girl was someone's 'girlfriend'. On rare occasions when the girl showed no particular interest in any one boy, she was labelled a 'lesbian' and all interest in her waned. The worse–case scenario was when a girl would identify two or three young men that she was interested in, but couldn't or wouldn't choose, and these boys were from rival gangs. When it was within one gang, the boys would sort it out between themselves based on their own pecking order, but when it was rival gangs, or one of the 'chosen' boys was not affiliated to any gang, fights would break out, even amongst those who had no chance with the girl. During these interludes it was difficult to keep the young people interested in their lessons, putting considerable stress on the teachers' resources while keeping the residential staff busy and the secure unit occupied.

Girls added a whole new set of complications to the routine of the school, not the least of these was around toileting. Quite early in my career at the Youth Justice School I discovered the convenience of going to the toilet upon request was more an opportunity to stash items pilfered from the school, rather than a need to relieve the bladder. Frequent requests to use the lavatory became a disruption technique used by the young people. As a consequence to this, set toilet times were built into the school's timetable. This allowed us to check all the resources before anyone left the school and meant minimum disruptions to the lessons.

The boys' toileting needs were met via the boys' wing which was attached close to the school, but the girls' toilet block was in the girls' wing at the other end of the complex. Any girl's request to go to the toilet had to be accommodated given that the girls needs differed from boys, taking into consideration their menstrual cycle. And girls had to be accompanied by a female social worker, which created another complexity. Each team of social workers included at least one female, but they were not always timetabled to be in the school. This sometimes necessitated my ringing through to the supervisor to request the attendance of a female staff member. A response was not always as prompt as we would have liked and the girl would become anxious. In this situation, against all the rules and putting ourselves at risk, Janice or I would ask one of the male social workers to supervise our group in the school room, and we would accompany the restless girl to the toilet.

A further complication was that the girls would fight, argue and socialise together in different ways to the boys. Rather than taking into account gang affiliations, setting the groups up in the morning also necessitated knowing what girls were in residence and who was talking, or not talking, to whom. The girls would come to school bearing the emotional and sometimes physical scars of some perceived relationship trauma that had occurred during the night. Their way of gaining the school staff's attention was also different from the boys. If they felt they were being neglected or ignored, the boys would use verbal or physical aggression to express their displeasure. In contrast, the girls would become emotional and burst into tears, scream accusations, sulk, or throw themselves onto the floor. In general, the girls took longer to settle into the school than the boys.

I recall one young lady who took exception to me from the moment I met her in the residential hall. I will give her the pseudonym 'Kitty' because she very much reminded me of a cat - a sleek, agile and fiery panther. Kitty was very vocal in her dislike of me and would share my pedigree with everyone within hearing. Her dislike was not gender specific - she communicated well with the other female staff - Kitty just didn't like me. Perhaps it was an age, authority or racial thing? Kitty not liking me was okay, because after a few days I didn't much like her either. I certainly didn't like her behaviour. In the mornings when she had maths with me, Kitty would grab her folder, refuse my offers of assistance and slump over to the assembly area where she would work alongside one of the social workers. During her second week in the school we had visitors: a judge, a lawyer and some other dignitary. Kitty was on the computers for the first part of the afternoon. She refused Janice's request to move at the end of the period so that another young person could have their turn. I approached her in the small space of the computer room and asked her to move. She exploded! The verbal abuse towards me was foul, but I persisted with the request for her to leave the computer room. Kitty threw herself off the chair and sprawled on the floor, swearing abuse while claiming I'd touched her. She leaped to her feet and slammed out of the computer room, her obscenities getting worse as she escalated. She spotted the visitors and rushed over to them, in a high-pitched voice screaming that I was hurting her; that I was "the cruellest, ugliest bitch under the sun" and should be fired. "Look, look!" she screamed, lifting her top up to show them her naked breasts, "I'm bruised where she hurt me and it was my fucking turn," (referring to the computer I assume). Galvanized by the display of breasts to visiting bigwigs, the social workers grappled with Kitty in an attempt to cover her up. It didn't work and she pushed them off, ripping her clothes in the struggle. Our very uncomfortable visitors discreetly left and within minutes Kitty, accompanied by several embarrassed social workers, was removed from the school.

On her return the next morning, Kitty meandered in, smiled at me for the first time, and was a model student for the rest of the day. I was suspicious and wary, watching her every move in anticipation of the next creative onslaught. But it never eventuated.

Kitty warmed to me, and I to her. This could be attributed to the medium of rug making. I was always on the lookout for some new skill and activity to introduce into the school in the afternoons, a complex process because of the security risks. Knitting was out because of the potential harm that could be inflicted from the long needles, and I was unwilling to compromise safety around sharp needles and scissors in sewing and embroidery. A rug making kit seemed perfect, with its pre-cut wool and small hook, but would any of the young people be interested? To my amazement some of the girls and a few boys latched onto it. The repetitive movement had a soothing effect on them, Kitty included. Once introduced to the skill of rug making, Kitty spent many afternoons working with the wool on canvas, creating a magnificent soft mat with a black and cream Siamese cat on a light blue background. She would curl up next to me or one of the female social workers, and pull the cut threads through the holes, chatting about this and that, whatever came to mind. In this way she began to share her stories of an abusive family and a bleak life on the streets.

By the time she left our school, I had grown to love this beautiful, traumatised child. Kitty never got to complete the cat rug. Instead several of the female social workers took it upon themselves to complete it for her. I kept the finished rug at the school until the last day, just in case she returned, but she never did.

JESSIE'S SECRET

At the residence's morning briefing, where the evening staff hand over to the day staff, it was announced that a girl had arrived during the night. For several weeks there had been only boys in the unit and the mood had been calm, with little altercation between members of rival gangs. I sighed in expectation of an unsettled few days ahead, as it was inevitable that the arrival of this girl would change the dynamics as the boys vied for her attention. Hearing my sigh, the residential supervisor chuckled. He reassured me that we would have no problems with this one; Jessie looked different. I wasn't so sure. How the girl looked had never bothered the boys before. Any similar-aged female was a prime target for their attention, providing them with justification to challenge and fight each other. I doubted that the girl's appearance would make a difference.

The young people were led into the school later that morning following the usual routine. Subdued, they sat in their semicircle in the assembly area and we went through the motions of greeting each other in a variety of languages. As was our custom, anyone could make a statement after the formal greeting. One of the boys yawned, stretched out his legs and stated in a bored manner that there was a new student, a girl. "Ugly as" muttered one of the other boys. "Yeah, ugly!" exclaimed another. Disappointment hung in the air, but at least they were settled.

Once the students were engrossed in their lessons under the supervision of the school and residential staff, I picked up my assessment kit from the office cupboard and walked down to where the new arrivals waited for their induction into the school. When I pushed open the double doors leading into the hall I saw what looked like a boy sitting alone on the low wooden bench. An adult stood apart, watching from a distance. There was no other student there. This had to be the new girl. She sat with her back straight against the wall. Her shiny bald head drooped onto her chest, giving an impression of a thick double chin. She had large ears that appeared misshapen by her lobes being dragged down with heavy metal earrings. My attention was drawn from her head to her purple tattooed hands that she placed flat on the knees of her worn, light blue denim dungarees, fingers spread widely. This was Jessie, then. I wondered why she was allowed to keep her earrings in. "Hi," I said, stepping closer and introducing myself by offering a hand in welcome. Hesitation. In slow motion she turned her head and looked up. I was shocked to see what must have been a tonne of metal rings, pins and rods hanging from her prominent nose, her eyelids and cheeks.

"Fuck off!" she snapped.

Oh great, it was going to be one of these starts. This was becoming a standard reaction with young people new to the facility. The more experienced youth bided their time and checked out the situation before they provoked those they perceived to be in authority. I waited a few minutes. "Mind if I sit down?" I enquired, trying to keep my voice as pleasant as I could. No response. At least it wasn't the usual 'no' with expletives. I sat down, respecting her space, and my safety, by ensuring there was a few feet between us. Neither Jessie nor I said anything for a while then, my voice soft, I explained the procedure for young people to enter the school. No response. Okay, I thought to myself, what category of student would I place this new girl. Hmmm, perhaps a passive resister? I took a surreptitious glimpse at her and noticed the cluster of silver balls protruding from her tongue. Unable to restrain myself, I got the giggles.

"What ya laughing at?" she snorted.

"Ever walked past a magnet?" I blurted out. She turned her head to the side and looked up at me. For the first time I noticed her dazzling blue eyes. She grunted, then let out a laugh. Now we were laughing together.

"I'm a dyke," she declared mid-laughter.

"Okay," I said.

"And the name's Jess."

"Right. Hello Jess, I'm Alison." This time she shook my hand. The assessment process was interrupted towards the end of our session by a visiting doctor. Jessie was about to lose all her body adornment.

Filing into the school room the following morning with the boys, minus the metal, Jess looked softer, vulnerable, a little bit more like a girl. But she was tough. Having declared her sexual preference with the staff and the youth with some authority, Jess blended into the school life without a ripple or an argument among the boys. She was intelligent, funny, a keen student and a pleasure to have around. There was the odd occasion when a boy would make a move on her and she would put him in his place by saying something cutting and personal. Sometimes, when she felt it necessary to emphasise her position and physical strength, Jess would use her fists. But this didn't occur often. Jess's knowledge and skill with verbal abuse, swear words and put-downs was phenomenal and effective. Soon other girls arrived which distracted the boys and even the biggest trier left Jess alone.

With the admittance of new girls to the residence, there was some concern about having a self-declared lesbian in the girls' wing. Adjustments were made to accommodate Jess in her own room away from the other youth. I suspect Jess enjoyed her isolation, keeping herself to herself and showing no interest in anything other than getting out of the residence and going home to live with her mother. She'd been living on the streets when she committed her crime and she wanted to return to the comfort of her family.

Jess was with us for over two months when her last day in the residence approached. The young people were never expected to attend school on their last day, but she sent a message to the school through one of the supervisors requesting permission to come and say goodbye. I met her in the foyer. She looked smart and tidy, almost pretty with her fluff of blonde hair, baby blue shirt and minus the metal jewellery. Jess introduced me to her mother, an attractive, rather elegant woman in her mid-thirties. I was pleased to note a warm affection between mother and daughter. As I held the exit door for them to leave together, Jess put her foot in the door, leaned over and said, with a twinkle in her eye, "I've got a secret".

"Oh," I said, "what is it?"

"I'm not a dyke." she laughed. "I lied. I tell them that to keep them off of me". Cool trick, eh?" And off she sauntered out the door to join her waiting mother on the driveway. Like I said, Jessie was an intelligent girl. I reckon she'll survive.

OSCAR

Oscar was different from the other young people. He arrived at the school with the label of being intellectually impaired. Oscar was a tall, obese but handsome boy with a happy, trusting disposition. Every morning he would bounce into the school and greet us warmly, reaching out his huge arms, asking for a cuddle. In return we would respond with warm refusals and smiles, and remind him of the 'no touching' rule. Oscar would give his big grin, repeat "no touching" and reach out for the next person. While he was a favourite with all the staff, what was surprising was how his peers tolerated him and his difference. Sometimes one of the boys would trick him to get a laugh, but I never saw him being bullied in an aggressive or cruel way. On the odd occasion when the trick confused or upset Oscar, someone would step in, give him a pat on the back or put an arm around his shoulders and reassure him. He'd respond with a "you're my friend," grin and attempt to give his saviour a hug.

Oscar loved to talk. Most of his talk was repetitive. He would wander around the school telling anyone who would listen that he was retarded. "I'm a retard," he would parrot as he skipped around the place, a large grin on his face. "I'm a retard 'cause my mum's boyfriend used my head for karate practice," he would share, over and over.

Every day was a new and exciting day for Oscar. He couldn't read and couldn't write his name, although he could recognise the 'O' for Oscar. I went to the local bookshop and purchased some picture books that I thought might interest him. Oscar was fixated on bikes, cars, trucks; any form of transportation with wheels. He didn't like rocket ships because they didn't have wheels. Although diagnosed as having Attention Deficit, Hyperactive Disorder, Oscar would sit for long periods on the floor poring over the pictures in the books or laminated cards we purchased or produced for him. "Look at this," he'd call out to no one in particular. "Look at this big red tractor with the great big wheels." It was the same picture that had entranced him the day before, and the day before that.

Curious about why Oscar was in the Youth Justice Residential facility, and why he kept coming back to us a month or two after being released, I checked his file. Oscar had been put into care as a toddler and had lived with a number of caregivers over the years. It appeared from his file that from the time he could walk, Oscar would help himself to other children's bikes. As he grew older he became more ambitious and would steal anything with wheels, including cars, motorbikes, vans and even a truck. Oscar talked about one day being able to drive a fire engine. To drive a fire engine was his greatest desire. Given that Oscar was a repeat offender; a repeat vehicle thief, I asked the supervisor why he was incarcerated among other young people who were considered violent.

Oscar never presented as being violent. He just stole vehicles. The supervisor handed me Oscar's second file. On one of his escapades, Oscar, who didn't have a licence and had never had formal driving lessons, drove into a woman on a crossing. I read that her injuries required extensive hospitalisation and it was anticipated she would be disabled for life.

Two years after the Youth Justice Residential Centre closed, I read in the newspaper that a young man had been killed in a car crash. It was Oscar. He had stolen a car, was the sole occupant, and while speeding crossed the centre line and hit an oncoming car. There were several fatalities; one was a child.

MANAGING THE ANGER

Luke was cool. He was tough. Luke was so tough, in his defiance he would come into the school without his shoes or socks. This meant we all got to see his dirty feet when he put them up onto the heavy coffee table that stood in the centre of our assembly area. Luke also had no social graces. He was gross. He'd pick his nose, rub it into his hands and wipe it on people. One of his favourite morning tricks was to hide the pickings in the palm of his hand and then shake your hand in greeting when he entered the school. Luke also had an anger management problem. If things didn't go his way he would have a tantrum; stamp his feet, yell, swear, rip things off the wall and lash out with his fists and bare feet. We developed a strategy for working with Luke. Learning to anticipate an eruption, rather than escalate him, we would smile, shrug our shoulders, and walk away from him to attend another young person. If Luke became too aggressive, the social workers would tackle him to the ground and hold him there until he stopped thrashing around. Then they would pull him up onto his feet, and with his arms behind his back, escort him out of the school. When he had calmed down, which sometimes only took ten minutes, they would return him and we would try again. In this way Luke learnt the ways of the school and stayed out of the secure unit.

By the time Luke joined us, we had updated 'No. 3' computer with the latest version of '*The Need for Speed*', the car racing game that was a favourite of many of the boys. Luke loved this game. Even though his behaviours had improved, he still had his off days. One of his off days was a particular Wednesday. He arrived in a bad mood and sat, sullen, on the couch, refusing to go with his group to their allocated table. He also refused to do any work when it was brought to him, throwing the folder and pencil onto the floor. No amount of encouragement or prompting worked with Luke on this Wednesday, so rather than evicting him from the school, we decided to ignore him. Luke did not like being ignored. To get our attention he muttered and screamed abuse, directed at no one person in particular. A social worker approached him and told him to stop his yelling. Luke got to his grubby feet and head butted the man. Two other social workers rushed to their colleague's assistance and the three of them tackled an enraged Luke to the ground. They put him into the appropriate position and dragged him towards the exit door that led to the boys' wing. Luke was in a fury, tearing at their clothes, kicking and crying. Somehow he untangled an arm and slammed his fist into the nearest wall. This happened to be the wall that backed on to the school's compact computer room. Computer No. 3 was on the other side of the wall nearest to Luke. As Luke struck the wall, computer No. 3 went down, and it stayed down for the rest of the day. This meant four computers, rather than the usual five, were now available during the afternoon option period. The other students were most put out. When Luke returned to the school that afternoon, his injured hand wrapped in a bandage, several boys blamed him for the loss of their favourite computer and game. To keep him safe from possible retaliation, Luke was sat at a table with a social worker for company. Filled with self-pity, he sulked all afternoon as he worked on the lessons he had missed that morning.

Luke's act of aggression offered an opportunity for a behaviour management lesson. When school was over I checked the damaged computer and found the problem – a loose electrical connection and an easy fix. I removed the cord and at assembly the following morning told the young people that the lead had been damaged by the thump to the wall. It would have to be repaired and the computer would be out of commission until Monday. It was a lie but it provided an interesting social experiment. At the Monday morning assembly I announced that all computers were up and running but I would appreciate that if anyone was going to have a melt-down, would they please avoid hitting or kicking the wall adjacent to the computer room. For the rest of the time that the school was open, no one ever became violent within the vicinity of the computers. In this way I determined that even when they were in a rage, the young people had some control over where they directed their anger.

OUR ARTIST

Buddy was one of those special people. A beautiful and talented young man. He came to us wrapped in an aura of serenity – calm, quiet, smiling and vague. He floated into the schoolroom. It turned out Buddy was a very talented drawer. Peter described him as a gifted artist. We all loved Buddy for the calmness that he brought with him, and because he loved to draw beautiful pictures that uplifted you. He spent many hours sketching out intricate pictures of natural objects. Buddy only drew natural, living things. Never people, animals or machines; mainly birds and fish, but also vibrant coloured shells. He would work his magic with the inexpensive coloured pencils we provided. You could almost feel the scales of the fish and the softness of the bird's feathers. I was especially entranced by the effervescent, colourful Paua shells Buddy drew.

Buddy came to us with a horrible story. While he never once mentioned it himself, we knew some of the details because Buddy was infamous. He had killed someone. It was something to do with a gang thing. The news media reported some male relative handing Buddy a weapon and ordering him to kill someone. Buddy had complied and now he was with us at the Youth Justice School. Because his story was splashed across the national newspapers and discussed on the radio, for the months he was with us we learnt to anticipate the time the news was being broadcast and turned the radio off. A few days before and after Buddy attended court, rather than having the radio on in the background, we played taped music to avoid hearing commentary about his crime or his fate.

Buddy's drawings were so exquisite that we displayed them around the walls of the school. They were taped alongside less talented but cherished exhibits created by other young people who had attempted to emulate Buddy's skills. Buddy's presence had brought an appreciation of art into our midst. I loved his drawings but we never had them for long. With envy I would watch as he retrieved a prized piece of his work from the wall and handed it over to one of his visitors in a gesture of appreciation. His lawyer was touched, quite teary, when Buddy presented him with an exquisite, detailed drawing of a kingfisher; its wet wing feathers gleaming against the stark whiteness of the inexpensive paper. The lawyer said he'd have his picture framed and would display it in his office. It was a beautiful treasure and I was pleased that Buddy valued his lawyer and was able to show his appreciation in this way. Those of us who worked in the school knew not to ask Buddy for one of his pictures. He never gave his work to anyone in the facility; it was always given away to someone from the outside. I guessed the motive behind this was that, unlike Buddy, his pictures were free to leave the Youth Justice facility.

Over the weeks Buddy's demeanour began to change. It showed first in his art. His use of colour became muted and seemed to fade away. The rich blues and greens were replaced by different shades of grey. He no longer asked for the red, orange or yellow pencils. A black pencil became his tool of choice. The focus of his drawings changed too. He no longer drew the beautiful lifelike birds, the shimmering fish or the cultured seashells. Nor did he offer his work for display or present it to his visitors. It became a private collection. Buddy created a folder of his work that he asked me to keep tucked away inside the school's locked office. Sometimes I caught a quick glimpse of his drawings and I would see dark shapes whirling out of mists, shadowy caves and unrecognisable flying things floating, hovering in the air. I imagined them as hawks, searching for their unsuspecting victims on the ground. If I hovered near Buddy while he was drawing or asked about his work, he would scoop up his materials and hug the paper to his chest. He would mutter some indistinguishable explanation, and move away from me to be by himself. Later, his drawings hidden from sight, a remnant smudging of lead would show on his shirt.

Buddy stopped smiling. Never one for talking much, now he wandered around the schoolroom, whispering in quiet tones, having private conversations with himself. Sometimes he would raise his voice and yell out to a person who wasn't there. Other times he would corner someone and ask them what hell was like. He asked me if I thought being in hell hurt. I answered what I thought at the time, "I don't know". That seemed to satisfy him and he walked away from me.

Buddy stopped drawing. The school staff were concerned for him but the social workers said they had it in hand. According to them a psychiatrist was visiting Buddy at the residence. Then one day Buddy stopped coming to the school. The other young people said he was staying back in his room because he wasn't well. I offered to take some school work to him but the social workers said it wasn't necessary as Buddy wasn't well enough to concentrate on lessons. Days went by. Buddy did not return to us.

One morning one of the boys came in and said Buddy was taken away during the night in an ambulance. Another boy said Buddy had "gone crazy, done a nutter and freaked out". None of the social workers seemed to know anything. I sought out their supervisor and he told me Buddy had been committed to a mental hospital but to keep it quiet.

Buddy never returned to our school. I sometimes wonder what became of him. I like to imagine that he is still drawing his beautiful pictures. That perhaps he is one of those gifted artists that work out of prison and become successful. I hope so because Buddy was such a beautiful person and such a talented artist.

EDUCATIONAL ASSESSMENT

A new routine was established. No young person would enter the school on their first day of being admitted to the Youth Justice Residential Centre. This process recognised the probability that new arrivals would be in an anxious state, and gave them a 'settling in' time to meet with the other young people. It also provided the advantage of giving the more established residents time to share with the new arrivals the culture and rules of the school, thus reducing incidents that might have required disciplinary procedures. On their second day every young person received an 'indoctrination' into the school. This began with a quiet chat with me in the residential hall, when the new arrival would be invited to participate in a reading, comprehension and mathematics assessment. I would explain the purpose of the assessment was to give school personnel an idea as to what level of work to give them at the outset. We did not wish them to be bored or patronised at school by giving work that was too easy, nor did we want them to become stressed by offering work that was too difficult. I would always speak of our school's motto: 'To try is to succeed'. This motto was displayed above the entrance to the school and was visible through the boys' wing window. From the first meeting an impression of choice was proffered: the young person could chose to comply with the request to do the assessments or could refuse to do the assessment and remain out of the school. If they felt they did not or could not face an assessment on that morning, I would thank them and promise to return the next morning. Later that same afternoon I would invite them on a tour of the school. During the tour they would meet the teaching staff and see the other young people participating in the electives. As I recall, no one, other than Peewee, ever chose to stay out of school longer than one day.

In those instances where a young person was returning to the school having been transferred back from another facility, I would ascertain their mood, greet them like long lost family, and where appropriate, invite them to join us in the school on that first day. This was easily accommodated because their assessment and achievement files were kept in the school office, along with several exercises that they could continue with if they returned to us. This system developed based on our experience that young people were removed from, and then returned to the Youth Justice residential centre at very short notice. When a young person had been gone a month, I would parcel up their certificates, type up a brief report on his or her achievements whilst in the school, and ask the relevant social worker (each young person had been allocated to a specific social worker) to send the parcel off to where-ever the young person had gone. But we always kept their file and new work ready, just in case.

The reading and comprehension assessments gave us an indication of the young person's reading age and their ability to cope with the written material placed in front of them. Often our students had a very limited knowledge of reading but where possible, the English teacher would prepare the young people for the 'New Zealand Practical Certificate in English'. The maths assessment was based on the Auckland Teacher's Training assessment package for determining the young person's level of skill in numbers, statistics, geometry and algebra. On their arrival each young person was assessed on their numbers and statistics skills. Once they had settled in they were given the choice of being assessed on the other two components as one of their electives or on the successful completion of a level in numbers or statistics.

Every young person had a maths folder of various colours. Colour choice was very important to the young people because of their gang affiliation. Giving someone who was associated with 'Black Power' a red folder would have dire consequences. I tried to keep a collection of folders in yellow, orange, green, brown and purple, avoiding red, white and blue where possible. Inside the front cover of their personal folder was glued a grid chart appropriate to the level of their ability. We always started with numbers by offering five worksheets across various skills at the level they were assessed at. I would sit with each new-entrant and, out of the hearing of others, would tell them the level that they were on for numbers and for statistics. The system we used was explained to them: they attempted the worksheet and could ask me, a social worker, or another student at their table for assistance. On completion the worksheet was marked and that element on the grid was blacked out. They were never given the same worksheet twice, and they were always given the choice of which of the five worksheets they would prefer to begin with. When any young person had a minimum of 30 worksheets blacked out, spread across the varying elements of that skill and level, they could call to sit an assessment test on the next school day. We had established high expectations and they were required to gain an accuracy of 80% to pass to the next level of numbers. As an alternative choice, they could opt to work on a statistics package to the level they had been assessed, or ask to sit the assessment tests for geometry and/or algebra. Where a young person achieved a mark of 75 to 79 percent, they were invited to sit with me and together we would go over their answers. During this session they were given the opportunity to 'talk to' some of their incorrect responses. When it was obvious that they knew the answer and it was an error in the processing of the problem, they were passed onto their next level. Those who did not achieve 75% or higher were given lessons and task sheets that addressed their weakness, and were invited to re-sit the assessment when they felt ready. The need to re-sit assessments rarely occurred as the young people elected to do the initial test when they were confident in a successful outcome.

In keeping with our motto 'To try is to Succeed', much was made of the young people who indicated that they wished to be assessed. When they made the call, everyone would fuss over them and I would make a grand display of putting together an individual assessment test ready for the next day. The assembly area, which was in a corner of the open plan schoolroom, was reserved for the young person and his or her 'exam supervisor', usually one of the social workers on duty. The student would indicate his or her readiness and the room would go quiet until the young person put down the pencil and handed me the completed paper. Most of the tests took about an hour to complete, however a time restriction was never put on the assessment test and would sometimes go into the next break. I believe that no student ever took an examination more seriously than the young people who attempted these tests in our school.

When a successful candidate moved up a level in their maths skills, the young person would be given a bonus of 50 points to spend on Friday afternoon, and we would all celebrate their success with congratulations. It became a matter of course that the other young people would slap the successful student on the back, give them the 'thumbs up' and show pleasure at the student's achievement. I would always reinforce the young person's success by explaining that once they had moved up a level, the knowledge could never be taken off them. This tended to be the norm, except for those who had been heavy drug users. What these young people learned over several days was often lost in 'blackouts' of memory, and so we would have to start again, re-teaching processes that had once been grasped. After several weeks, sometimes a month or two of being drug free, it became noticeable that learning would begin to 'stick and stay'.

Given the positive response to their successes, we were always on the lookout for new opportunities to offer the young people. The greatest barrier to this was the Youth Justice Residential Centre's 'high-risk security' status that meant not one of the young people was allowed off site or out of doors. Opportunities had to be created within the small, very constricted space of the school. Another barrier was the young people themselves. There was a general lack of motivation. It seemed easier to tough it out and refuse to participate than to suffer the humiliation of failing. What we needed was a 'hook' to motivate the young people to learn. This required research. We turned to the young people and asked them what they wanted to learn.

Despite a number of them having committed driving offences that included driving without a licence, there was a genuine desire to gain their driver's licence. We decided to use this incentive and brought in two sets of copies of the 25 'scratch-your-answer' questions that the Ministry of Transport used to test driving theory. One set had the correct answers scratched out and was laminated; the other set was laminated with the answers covered over. Those who were interested in going for their theory could elect to practice their questions in the afternoon session, self-marking or marking each other as they went. This technique was reinforced with a set of 10 copies of the road code and a computer software package put out by the Ministry of Transport. We found a motivated young person who had poor knowledge of even the most basic words would study the road code for hours. I have never seen students study so hard, for so long. They had that road code off by heart.

When the first group indicated they were ready, a local traffic officer was invited onto the site to examine them. Five young men who met the age criteria of being at least 15 years old opted to be the first to try for their theory test. Knowing their reaction to authority, especially someone in uniform, I was apprehensive as we walked through the boys' wing and into the Youth Justice Administration corridor to meet with the traffic officer (I had checked that the doors were all locked before we left the school). I need not have worried. All five were on their best behaviour and the officer treated them with politeness and an element of paternal courtesy. He explained that they would each be given one of the 25 'scratch-your-answer' sheets and they could make no more than three errors in total, or two from the back page. He sat them apart and allowed them each to draw from a selection of the sheets. I was invited to stay in the room but had to be quiet. This was awful to watch. A bundle of nerves, I trembled as the boys commenced the test. Each time a wrong answer was revealed I cringed but kept a smile plastered on my face.

They had been prepared for possible failure but all five passed this first crucial stage. Worse was to come. The officer sent us out of the office to wait in the secure corridor, calling each young person in one at a time to examine the oral component of the theory test. This involved five questions drawn from any section of the road code. Not being in the room with them, I had no idea how they were doing, although if I listened hard, I could hear voices through the door. Those waiting in the corridor with me never said a word; we were all too busy listening. All their intensive study had prepared them well. As each boy came out of the office, I knew that he had passed by his physical demeanour and the big smile spread across his face. I am sure that each one of them grew another inch or two in height that day. After all five had been tested, the traffic officer invited them back into the office and congratulated them on their success. He wrote out a form for each one and asked them to sign it. He then asked where they would like the documentation sent. This caused some confusion, as nobody knew where he would be in a week's time. In the end they elected to give their individual home addresses or the home of a relative. No one wanted his or her certificate sent to the residential centre, although this option was offered to each of them.

After the theory test, an interesting thing occurred on our way back to the schoolroom. This same thing was to occur on every occasion after a group of young people had sat and passed their driving test theory. As they walked through the boys' wing, their demeanour changed again. Without any prior discussion, each young person slumped forward that little bit, their eyes dropped and their faces took on a mask-like façade. I unlocked the school door. One behind the other, they walked past me and into the school. Those who had been waiting for their return looked up, questioning. Not wanting to ruin the moment, I avoided everyone's eyes, turned and locked the door behind the last young person in the line. Together the five boys walked into the room and then they lifted their heads, smiled at their audience and one boy gave the thumbs up. "Piece of cake." he said.

The place ignited as everyone gathered around them, congratulations flew around the room, backs were slapped, jokes were made about doing their practical component and the possibility of 100 points was negotiated. Their success became everyone's success, including the support staff in the reception area and in the dining room. These five beautiful, brave young men became celebrities for a day.

EXTERNAL EXAMINATIONS

With each new success the school staff became more ambitious and decided to offer the young people the option of sitting external examinations. The Unit Standards were new innovations in the New Zealand educational scene at this time and given that they could be taught in short blocks of time, we determined that they would be appropriate for our setting and useful to our young people. For our first trial, we selected unit standard 504 – 'Creating a Curriculum Vitae'.

Before and during the time I was at the Youth Justice School, I was also the New Zealand Director of the Primary Research Project and the Asia Wise Competition. Both of these programmes consisted of a 40 multi-choice examination that called on individual's research skills. Attempting either programme resulted in a certificate that indicated one's level of success, from 'Participation' to a 'Pass', through to a 'Merit', 'Distinction' and for the top 5% in New Zealand, a 'High Distinction'. We decided to trial these programmes in our school, commencing with the Primary Research Project that targeted children in Years seven and eight (pre-high school). All of our young people in the school at this time were invited to participate. They could work alone or in groups for four hours across three days. The purpose of the programme was to find the correct answer using research techniques. This included asking each other and the staff, making phone calls (we did this as a group with the candidates looking up phone numbers, me doing the dialling from the school's phone and an elected young person doing the questioning), sending faxes, linking one computer to the Internet, and searching the encyclopaedias, books and magazines we had on the school shelves or purchased. To maintain their self-respect, we told the young people that the 'primary' referred to the 'first' research project, as opposed to being directed at primary school students. The success gained from participating in this programme was significant. Not only did several students gain a distinction, but they also had a lot of fun working in collaboration or in competition against each other. The benefit of my being the New Zealand Director was that they could have their papers marked and returned within the week, which gave the satisfaction of prompt feedback and success whilst most of the participants were still in the residence.

It was during the Primary Research Project that I experienced one of those 'moving moments' that was an intrinsic reward for working in such a risky and stressful environment. We had one very large, heavy, rectangular coffee table in the school. Painted with splashes of many colours to camouflage and discourage graffiti and tagging, it was the central feature of our carpeted assembly area. On this day a group of young people, with staff permission, had moved it so they could get natural light from the north facing windows. There were six research papers opened on the table with eight people on their knees, leaning on the table reading the questions and discussing the answers. Their heads close together, in serious discussion around the merits of each answer, were a Maori male and female social worker, the shaved scalp of a 'skinhead' and young people from opposing gangs and ethnicities. Their differences and animosities set aside, they were all engrossed in their common goal. Watching them working together in harmony, tears stung my eyes and I had to turn away so that my emotions wouldn't draw attention to, or distract from, the moment. When I looked up I saw that Janice had also caught the moment and she too had tears in her eyes. We smiled and left them to it.

Almost all of the young people, thanks to Janice, had gained credible keyboarding skills. I approached the Director of the Pitman's Examinations in New Zealand and applied for the school to be registered as a special centre. Permission was granted based on my teaching qualifications and the agreement that, where possible, we would bring in an outside examiner. Many of our young people were to succeed in gaining their very first external qualification through this wonderful organisation. One or two of our 'longer termers' took up the challenge and became pioneers in preparing for, attempting and passing some of the more challenging examinations that Pitman's offered, including 'Practical Word Processing', 'English for Office Skills' and 'Commercial Numeracy'.

There was always the possibility of failure when the young people were entered into external examinations and we were very careful to prepare them for this event and to celebrate their efforts rather than to emphasize their achievements. Failures did occur but I do not recall any 'behavioural incident' that surrounded this. Despite our preparations, I rather suspected that our young people never expected to succeed and that failure was their expected outcome. This was reinforced when the occasional incident occurred around a student's success. Unfamiliar with achieving and the emotions this evoked, when some of the young people were informed they had passed the examination they would act out. On one occasion an angry young man accused me of fixing the results as he had never passed a test before. Their success created other problems, such as what to aim for now, and what to do with their certificates. Original certificates kept by the young person in his or her room created a risk as another person might remove or damage it. This led to accusations and fights. Given a variety of options, including sending the certificates home, most of the young people directed me to keep certificates secure in their file and to give or post it to them when they left. A satisfactory solution was established where we photocopied the original and gave the successful student the copy to keep on his or her person. Sometimes we would get a request for the original so that the young person could show his/her family or lawyer, or to present it at a Family Group Conference.

Many of the young people developed a close bond with their assigned residential social worker. This was especially true for those who were in the centre for months. They almost always wanted to show this person what they had achieved and to give them a copy of their certificate for their file. It was in the last months at the school that I began to appreciate the role that the social workers played beyond that of providing security. Many of these professional adults cared about the young people in their care and they often demonstrated a supportive parental role. The pride they felt when their young people achieved often showed and this enhanced the young person's success.

Skills as well as academic success were encouraged through the school. An experienced welder was brought in to teach interested young people the basics of arc and gas welding and cutting. As could be expected, one of the first questions to the tutor was "how do you open a safe?" This was always met with amusement by the specialist but was threatening to some of the onlookers. It was during this period that I was informed by a senior member of the residential staff that the young people were better off being kept illiterate, as "an educated criminal is a lot more dangerous to society than an ignorant one". School personnel never adhered to this philosophy. What knowledge we had access to was always offered to, and shared with the young people. We never withheld information from a young person because of fear of what use it could be put to when they left the residence.

PRINCE CHARMING

There was something about Chance. Something about him put people at their ease. You felt you could trust him. The first time I approached Chance was in the residential hall. He stepped towards me with his hand held out in invitation. Looking me in the eye, smiling his warm greeting, he shared how pleased he was to meet me. With his handsome appearance and pleasant manner, he was eloquent and charming. Smooth. Certainly not our norm.

At my invitation Chance completed the entry assessment. When this was completed to his satisfaction, at his request we meandered together through the hallway and into the school. Later that evening, when marking his assessment papers, I was surprised and delighted to discover a true scholar. Chance gained one hundred percent on all the tests. Not only was he charismatic, Chance was intelligent. He also proved to be a natural leader.

Whatever Chance said the others would follow. Of mixed ethnicity, he appeared not to affiliate with any specific group or gang. This lack of association seemed to enhance his popularity among the residents rather than diminish it. Chance's presence in the school brought an aura of peace. He was always respectful towards the teaching staff and acted as a peacemaker when other students became antagonistic. There did not appear to be a criminal or malicious bone in his body. Not having looked at his records, I did wonder what crime this charming young man could have committed that resulted in him being 'under supervision' in the Youth Justice facility. Reflecting on this, I determined that it would be better not to know. We would take Chance at face value and enjoy his company and positive influence in the school.

One of the teachers became unwell and we welcomed a new relieving teacher into our midst; a young woman on maternity leave.   Knowledgeable, experienced and vivacious, with the confidence of youth Gemma marched into the school. Straight into the arms of Chance. They hugged and greeted as if old friends, which indeed they were. We were all rather flabbergasted by this display of familiarity. From snippets of their conversation I ascertained that Gemma had been Chance's teacher in his Intermediate years (years 7 and 8) four years earlier. Beaming, her arms still around a grinning Chance, Gemma declared he had been a favourite of hers. "So bright, so much potential", she declared.   "I just loved him".   I suggested we have a chat in the office and directed Chance towards his group at the English table. Still grinning, he complied. This young lady stayed with us for several days, but became uncomfortable due to the attentions of another young man and so we didn't invite her back.

On entry to the unit, Chance reported he was in the sixth form (year 12) and had gained a number of passes in School Certificate the previous year. Having a student who had achieved academic success was a rarity in the school and the teachers enjoyed the challenge of creating lessons at his level, seeking to advance his learning. One day I approached him about his area of interest and expertise. He was a little vague about his subjects and grades and so I rung the secondary school he said he attended before his arrest. They had never heard of him. No one of that name had ever attended their school. Chance had either lied about the college he had attended, or lied about his name. Because the relieving teacher knew him by the name we had on our records, it was probable that Chance attended a different secondary school to the prestigious one he had listed. I rung around the schools in the area he lived and soon discovered Chance had dropped out of school two years earlier; he had never sat or passed any School Certificate examinations. Rather than confront Chance with this new information, the school staff decided to keep it to ourselves. We agreed to concentrate on the strengths in literacy and mathematics that he had demonstrated in the initial assessments. With his permission we commenced preparing him for the external Pitman's Examinations, which he excelled in.

An astute young man, I believe Chance knew that he had been found out in his lie. A model student, he continued to charm and support the school staff throughout his stay at the Youth Justice residence. When he turned 17 Chance was transferred to an adult prison to complete his sentence. We were informed by his social worker that Chance had committed serious offences against very young children.

THE WELDER'S STORY

Many of the young people were tactile learners and we were always looking for opportunities to bring skilled tradesmen into the school to pass on some of their knowledge. One of the staff was related to a man who had considerable experience and expertise as a toolmaker, fitter and turner, and who was now self-employed. He was asked if he would develop a course that would be suitable for young people in a secure facility. He offered to teach them the basics of welding.

This is his story:

"When they asked me to come into the youth justice school and teach some of the young people, I thought it would be a challenge. I wasn't nervous about working with young offenders because I've worked with many apprentices over the years and trained them. A few of them had been troublemakers but this was never a problem because I'm very large; over 6' 5' and weigh over 120 kilos. I've probably always been bigger than them and they normally respect, look up to me, well physically they have to at least.

The principal at the school asked me to design a course that would teach the young people a skill. I've trained many apprentices over the years through the time I was at this large International factory and I thought it would just be an extension of that but in a more controlled environment. The fact they were all violent offenders wasn't a problem at all. The only difference that I thought of was that I didn't know if these young people wanted to learn or if they were being forced to learn. An apprentice wants to learn because he wants to learn a trade. I thought that maybe the young people at the Youth Justice facility would only be doing it to fill in time rather than actually trying to learn a skill.

I thought about the course and what I could teach them and decided on gas fusion welding, which is just using oxygen/acetylene mix, welding steel to steel, common metals with a filler rod. I could teach them easy flowing which is welding dissimilar metals, again using oxygen and acetylene. I'd introduce them to silfosing which is joining copper to copper, and bronze welding which can be used for a multitude of different materials you can weld together. Things that are quite simple to do if you listen to the basic instructions. Also maybe gas cutting which is cutting steel using oxygen/acetylene with a special torch, and arc welding. I didn't bother teaching them soldering, they could always do that later, or mig or tig welding because we didn't have the equipment. In designing the course, I had to take into account all the safety aspects, like what safety equipment would be needed, and the clothing that they wore in the facility. Usually they didn't wear shoes in the school for security reasons, but I insisted on heavy safety shoes if they were on the welding course. There was to be no jandals, or bare or stockinged feet in the welding room. The first lesson would be about safety, things like the danger of having their eyes burnt by the intense light and why we used special shades of welding glass in the helmets, prevention of risks such as electrical shocks and fire.

The course was to be for two mornings a week for eight weeks so we didn't have time to do everything. I'd arrive at 9 am to set up and leave when the young people went to lunch. My first visit to the facility was out of normal hours. I was invited in, shown the room and asked if it would be suitable. The room wasn't very large, it was probably about three metres by two metres wide, had a bench down one side, had a half set of cupboards down the other and a wooden door with a Georgian wire glass window in it, clear, which the school room and office could look in which was good because the social workers could stand on the outside looking in. I didn't want them inside the small space with us. There was a dust extraction unit in the room because it had been used as a bone carving room in the past. It had a linoleum floor which was already in poor condition so it didn't matter if some sparks or a bit of hot metal landed on the floor. It wouldn't do any damage; wouldn't set fire to the place. I remember the room was really dusty so we had to clean it first. All we needed in there was basically a small school desk and most of the stuff was set up on that. The oxy bottles were set up on a trolley, the arc welder I brought in each time we placed on a chair, or on a bench next to it and we just ran the leads or the hoses out. It worked out really well. And there was also a fire-hose reel that was just outside the door so if anything major happened we had access to it. I deliberately did not take a fire extinguisher in there because of the potential problems with the young people playing or discharging it.

I used all my own equipment, bringing it in every day. The facility provided the water for the bucket and the students. That was it. I used two very small bottles with the oxygen and acetylene; the smallest you could get. The gauges and regulators and hoses were all on a trolley and had to be wheeled in. I had a special arc welder, a very small arc welder which was ideal because I could carry it under one arm, made two or three trips with the welding rods in one hand and the steel in the other and just came backwards and forwards. It only took a couple of minutes to set up but it was critical for obvious reasons that all the welding rods were counted when I arrived and before I left. Everything had to be accounted for.

I remember the first day when I met the young people. There was a group meeting of those who wanted to do the course. Over half of them there at the time wanted to do the course, and three of these were girls. The school staff decided who could do it and I took these aside, met all of them and gave them a rundown of what it was all about, gas cutting, arc welding; all the different styles they would be learning. Some of them jumped at the idea, got excited because they suddenly thought, gas cutting, hey we could break into safes when we know how to gas cut. The social workers got a bit nervous but I said "yeah fine, I'll teach you how to gas cut". Boy, were those kids motivated. And later, at the end of the course I explained to them how a modern safe worked. I said "you're wasting your time trying to gas cut into a safe, you'll never do it. The only way you'll get into a safe today is to find the combination. But at least you've learned a skill". Some of them were a bit taken aback about being fooled, but they all appreciated that they could now gas cut and they had skills their mates didn't have.

Having steel around young people who were all violent offenders was a bit of a problem for the staff. It didn't turn out to be a problem though because I told the young people when we first started that there was a big bucket of water there and if they set fire to themselves, I'd throw the bucket of water over them to put it out. The bucket was there for a purpose. When we finished doing any gas cutting or stopped using welding rods that got too short, they'd have to go into the bucket to be cooled down. Also if the young person put their hand in the bucket I could see water on their fingers so I knew they'd taken something out of it. That was my back-up. Having a large, deep bucket so the hot steel and the off-cuts dropped to the bottom, so if a person put their hands in they would come out with wet hands and you could see that for up to a minute or two later and you'd know what they'd been up to. It was about being alert, keeping an eye on them.

We set it up that there would be a maximum of two young people in the room at any one time. I was by myself with them while a social worker stood outside watching through the window. Except for when we were arc welding. I insisted that a social worker be inside the room with us when I was demonstrating arc welding, because if I had an arc welding helmet over my face, and the person that I'm teaching has an arc welding helmet over his or her face, the other student in the room can be doing anything or walking anywhere. The social worker had to be in there, without a helmet on, watching the second student. When we were just gas cutting or gas welding, I could see what they were up to the whole time. The social workers were quite vigorous in coming in, they wanted to learn as well, they were really interested, but I just could not teach them at the same time. I was there for the young people. The hardest part of the course was getting the social workers to keep their eyes on the young people but they kept getting bored. They'd be there for hours at a time, doing nothing but watching, they couldn't do anything physically themselves and they wanted to get their hands on the equipment, but that wasn't part of their job. I had more problems with the social workers touching things than the young people.

Every day I kept a register of what the young people had been taught and who was in on that particular day and block so we knew they were all being given equal time. Because we were using steel and welding rods and razor sharp bits of steel, we couldn't make anything for them to take out of the school. It would be too dangerous as it could be used as weapons or for picking locks. So we'd gas cut profiles and shapes out, we welded steel together to make it look like guards or different machinery, letterbox type things, and then we'd cut them up or use a disk grinder to break them up and use that same metal for the next part of the class. They all realised they weren't allowed to take it out of the welding room and they were quite happy to see how things went together and how it came apart again. A lot of the tests we did, especially fusion welding, we actually tried to destroy the welds to show them how strong the welds were. We'd hammer the stuff and bend it backwards and forwards until we fatigued the metal or until it snapped. Most of time the parent metal would snap and never the weld. They loved it and were always keen. It was satisfying work. Great students.

Once a couple of boys started clowning around a bit with the gas torch and I gave them a practical demonstration of how easy it would be for me to set them on fire. They suddenly realised that you don't fool around with welding equipment and how dangerous it is. Like I said, I'm physically a lot bigger than them, stronger, and they didn't want to push their boundaries so they quickly settled down. It was good, we got on very, very well. There were no problems at all. One girl stood up suddenly under the cabinet on the wall and damn near knocked it off. I thought she'd knocked herself out but she surprised me. Just shook her head and said "that hurt". I said she'd make a damn good scrum forward with a head that hard. She laughed and just got on with the job. Really impressive.

On another occasion two of the boys were tickling each other, being stupid, dangerous, so I invited them to have a go at me. As they came towards me I swung around with the gas torch. It was aimed above their heads but they realised how quickly their eyebrows could have been burnt off so that sort of kept them in their place. They were actually really well behaved. All of them. If they did play up they just got told they'd be shown the door and that was it. They were happy to be there. It broke their day and they were learning a skill, and I was more than happy to pass on my knowledge. The facility was only 15 minutes from my workshop that I worked out of and I could programme my workload to suit. I was happy to come in and do this type of work.

Once a couple of boys played up a little bit but it was just a matter of talking with them, convincing them of the error of their ways and if they didn't want to learn, they could walk out the door there and then, and those who did want to learn could stay on and I'd spend a lot more time with them. They all stayed right to the end and everyone passed the complete course. Things like the gas fusion welding, most of them picked it up quickly because it is quite easy to do. The gas cutting was picked up quickly too, so was the silfosing as it's easy to do once you learn the basic principles. The hardest part of the course was arc welding. Some people have a natural flair for it and others haven't. That part of the course some just had to persevere. I'd explain to them where they were going wrong and explain in advance where I suspected they may find difficulties and show them how to correct it. Every person was different, their learning ability and speed. If a person picked it up you didn't keep them doing it repetitively. You'd stop them when they had a success, when they're happy and they've achieved so they went out on a high. If you keep them going they had a habit of deteriorating the work slightly and then they'd get upset. It's all in the timing and the knowing.

So did the young people think it was worth it? I think one or two of the boys and one girl seemed really keen on keeping on with the welding once they got out. The girl, I think her name was Jess or Jessie, something like that. Said she wanted to join the army and she said it was a good skill to take with her. She said she felt she had the basic training to carry on with whatever the army life had for her now. That was the same girl who almost knocked herself out. The boys, they weren't really sure why they wanted to learn welding, they just wanted a skill. And we talked about things like their mates' cars and their exhausts breaking off. This skill meant they had the ability to repair it for their mates, to save their mates paying good money out. And they liked welding copper pipes together. It's quite legal to have a still in New Zealand. They could make their own spirits. They knew how to make their own stills now, how to do the basic engineering work for them. Two of the boys were keen about following it through once they got out of the facility. But once they're out, we don't know where their mind's going to, what they'll get up to, but at least they have the basic training if they want to pursue it. At least they weren't bored, it gave them something to focus on while they were there and they learnt a new skill, something their mates didn't have. They'd have their certificate that they were presented with when they passed their course. They could go to a future employer and say, "look I've done a basic welding course, I know how to gas cut, arc weld, I know how to bronze, easy-flow, do silfos. I've done a welding course and passed it". It is only the introduction to it but at least they are one step ahead of the next applicant who hasn't got that skill. So that would put them a little bit ahead if they're looking for a job. I think that's what a lot of them realised, it gave them something that others didn't have.

It's not just the young people - I got something out of it too. I'd spent many years as chief engineer at a large International factory and trained a lot of apprentices. I was given really good training in my apprenticeship and this was a way of paying back something and I enjoyed passing my knowledge on. I have a lot of knowledge and I'm frightened that the knowledge will disappear when I go. By sharing it around, we may get some replacement tradesmen following through.

When I first saw the facility I was horrified by some parts of it. From the outside you could see the whole facility was in a bad state of repair. Inside I only ever saw the school, the welding room and the office. One day I was sitting outside waiting for the door to open. I started looking at the security screens around the windows to see how they'd been built. Just passing the time the way an engineer does. I started counting the screws that were holding the security screens in. Every security screen only had two screws in it. Someone had been around and removed the rest. These were security screens holding lexon type glass or polycarbonate which is meant to be shatter-proof. But someone had gone around on the outside and removed all the screws so that if a young person broke the window from the inside, put their boot to it, all the window screens would pop out and they could run down the street. I went into the school and told the principal and she got hold of the manager of the whole facility and he came out and had a look. Panic stations. They didn't know how it had happened or how long it'd been like that. They didn't know what to do. I said, "Your problem mate, not mine. I've just reported what I've seen".

My impression of the school though was that it was safe. They had big heavy tables that couldn't be picked up and thrown. The gas heater had a big steel cage around it. The teachers, two in particular I remember quite well, one was quite a character and fun to be with. The other one, the Englishman, a younger teacher, I got on well with him. There was a woman who spent a lot of time with the young people in the computer room or in the office, real friendly, always smiling. The principal, she was a dedicated and exceptionally skilled teacher. She would say that education is the way for these young people to move on with their lives and leave offending behind them. She saw education as more than bookwork, saw that the young people could learn from other people's experience and knowledge. The teachers, they were different people but they all got on well, you could see they respected each other. I remember several of the social workers too. They seemed to change quite regularly and I never knew who was on duty and who wasn't. But I enjoyed it. I enjoyed it all and regretted that the course couldn't continue because they closed it down and moved too far away.

Really this facility wasn't too bad compared to the new one that I saw later with its huge, high walls and horrible setting. Here the building was nicer, an older style building. I think the young people felt they weren't too far away from an ordinary community. There were houses around and there were nice green areas, and the hills. They could look out the windows and see up to people's houses. It was like they were in a normal sort of setting. Not in a huge, block prison."

CLOSING THE SCHOOL

There had been rumours floating around the residence and the community for some time, so I was not surprised when informed officially that the Youth Justice Residential Centre and its attached school were to close. Because of the severity of the young people's crimes, it was considered inappropriate to detain them within a residential housing community and the facility was moving to more secure premises further north. While I had hoped to move with the young people, I was told that my services as head teacher/principal were no longer required. The residential manager explained to me that education by trained teachers was to be replaced by programmes provided by people from within the local community. We were given several months to prepare and continued to work as a team right up until the day the doors were closed and the last of the young people were transported out to their new facility.

While the last day was very sad for the school staff, we also celebrated with the young people, knowing they would be going to a larger, new and more suitable facility with lots of space, specialized teaching areas and best of all, a state-of-the-art outdoor area. As well as putting on a morning tea, we finished with speeches and a 'special gift' for each young person: a positive affirmation for them to take away. The young person was invited to stand, then the school staff shared with him or her something we perceived was 'special' about them. Tears flowed amongst us, not only from the young person but from all the staff. In the final few minutes of our time together, the rule of 'no touching' was broken. We hugged, hands were shaken, backs and arms were patted and I even recall receiving an impetuous kiss on the cheek.

This then, was my last memory of the Youth Justice Residential School. It was heart breaking, as I had grown to love and respect our very special, sometimes bad, mostly sad, young people.

After the Youth Justice Centre and attached school closed, the school staff went their separate ways. I spent a year as a fixed-term assistant principal at an integrated post-primary school for girls, followed by a brief stint as a relieving teacher at an exclusive private girls' school. This experience was sufficient for me to realise that I felt an affiliation for, and preferred working with, young people, especially boys, from less advantaged backgrounds. I applied for and gained a position as 'Special Education Adviser' for New Zealand's Ministry of Education 'Special Education Services' (SES, who later became known as GSE; Group Special Education). My primary role in this relatively new position was to support children who exhibited severe, challenging behaviours in the mainstream classroom. It was like coming home.

REFLECTION

When I worked at the Youth Justice Residential Centre School, I participated in, observed, and experienced the transfer of knowledge. An aura of calmness and self-acceptance settled over the school as the young people began to reach out for and achieve success. These successes were just small steps. In the school each young person was on an individual programme where they were able to measure their own progress. But it was more than the school environment that added to their wellbeing. The residential facility also offered them nurture, structure and security. Free choice was replaced by certainty and routine. The young people no longer had to make decisions about whether they would do what was required of them. Wholesome and plentiful food was provided at regular times (often the 'long termers' gained weight) and the young people had their own clean beds, private room (albeit a small cell) and blankets. For those who had been surviving on the streets, this was luxurious.

While I expected there would be some resentment towards being incarcerated against their will, what I observed, on the most part, was a general sense of taking some 'time out' and relief from the lifestyle they had been living. They would settle within a few days of being placed in the facility, despite the occasional eruptions of aggression around them. Provided any young person who 'acted out' was removed, the others would settle into their routine. An episode of 'acting out' resulted in temporary removal from the school environment until the individual felt able to return. Once calm they could return to their table without further repercussion. The 'acting out' was recognised as being a simple 'hiccup of the moment'; an impulsive act, and did not lead to punishment or recriminations. Sometimes embarrassed and apologetic (never remorseful), the young person would return to the school, no explanation expected, required or asked for. It was enough that they were back amongst us.

Now that I am again working in the mainstream schools with students exhibiting challenging behaviours in the classroom, I reflect back on the extraordinary resource that was provided in the Youth Justice Residential Centre School – having someone to remove the troubled young person, take him or her away for a short period so that calmness could again prevail, and then return the now settled youth so that she or he could blend back into the classroom. What bliss. If mainstream schools were set up to work in this way, fewer children would be sent home to their frustrated, often bewildered parents and, I suspect, there would be a dramatic decrease in the number of suspensions, stand-downs and exclusions. Using this system, there was never a need to punish, to chastise or humiliate what are often very troubled children and adolescents. It was simply accepted that the young person needed to vent his or her emotions, albeit in a way that was unacceptable for the environment. So just remove them temporarily, talk to them, better still, listen to how they are feeling and try to offer them other ways to respond that is more acceptable. The feelings they are experiencing and unable to control are punitive enough for the child involved, why increase their unhappiness and their angst? Talk through the issue, try to resolve it, teach them to move on. That is what works; that is what will make the difference.

In the Youth Justice Residential facility, consistent routine was imperative. The young people needed to know the system, how it worked, when and why things happened. They also needed to know they had a voice. Opportunities had to be provided where they could vent their feelings; tell their side of the story. It was all about listening to them.

The young people in this book are on a journey. Their time in the Youth Justice Residential Centre was merely a stage in their journey and a life of crime and a prison cell is not necessarily their destination. Research and personal life experience have taught me that events, both planned and unexpected, can alter our life's course. Employment opportunities, affection, children, education, a place of belonging, all of these can make a difference.

I believe this book is more than a collection of stories. It reflects a model of education that worked for these special young people, the majority of whom were alienated, not only from the school system, but also from the wider community.

Is there an answer to the problem of youth offending? From my perspective and experience the answer for some young people on the pathway to offending, is a resounding YES! Well-run, well-resourced, long-term residential schools, with measures in place to ensure the young people are safe from predatory or abusive adults, will make a positive difference. We already see the effectiveness of existing residential schools for children with challenging behaviours, but they are too short term for the positive changes that occur to take hold. What I am advocating is what already exists for the children of the well-off in our community: a long term, well-financed, specialised boarding school system with holidays and long weekends spent with their families.

Prevention is preferable to punishment. Such a system could be created to cater for our most at-risk young people, targeting those aged eight to twelve years of age. Successful students could then be financed and integrated into established mainstream boarding or local secondary schools on graduation. Is it not more cost effective to build schools for our at-risk young people, than prisons for our alienated, uneducated adults? Education gives more than knowledge - it offers skills, opportunity, self-esteem, goals, and hope. It offers the young people a means to belong. And that is what our sometimes bad, mostly sad young people want. To belong.

'Tis education forms the common mind;
Just as the twig is bent the tree's inclined.
(Alexander Pope, Moral Essays)

EPILOGUE

During my time as principal/head teacher at the Youth Justice Residential Centre School, I repeatedly heard the same stories from the young people: "we mostly didn't like primary school, and we especially hated secondary school". I would sit amongst them and listen to the stories that reflected their alienation from the compulsory education system. When the residential facility closed and I began working with children exhibiting severe behaviours within the mainstream school setting, I found that many of their experiences were reflecting the same stories of the young people in the Youth Justice system. Was it possible that children who exhibit severe, challenging behaviours in school are on the pathway to youth offending?

To ascertain if there was a connection between children who presented with problematic behaviours within the school setting and future criminal offending, I turned to the academic literature. Frustrated by the lack of information on criminal offenders' compulsory school experience, I embarked on my next challenge – collecting the stories of the young people in the criminal system about their compulsory school experience. To listen to them and give a voice to their stories. The end result was my Ph.D. and a book of young offenders' stories: *'Classroom to Prison Cell'*, published in 2007.

www.ingramcontent.com/pod-product-compliance
Lightning Source LLC
Chambersburg PA
CBHW072137280526
45788CB00002B/669